Questions
Jesus Asked

Questions Jesus Asked

Questions Jesus Asked
978-1-7910-2688-2
978-1-7910-2782-7 *eBook*

Questions Jesus Asked: DVD
978-1-7910-2785-8

Questions Jesus Asked: Leader Guide
978-1-7910-2783-4
978-1-7910-2784-2 *eBook*

Also by Magrey R. deVega

Awaiting the Already:
An Advent Journey Through the Gospels

Embracing the Uncertain:
A Lenten Study for Unsteady Times

Savior:
What the Bible Says about the Cross

The Bible Year:
A Journey Through Scripture in 365 Days

With April Casperson, Ingrid McIntyre, and Matt Rawle
Almost Christmas:
A Wesleyan Advent Experience

MAGREY R. DEVEGA

Questions
JESUS ASKED

Abingdon Press | Nashville

Questions Jesus Asked

Library of Congress Control Number: 2022947382

978-1-7910-2688-2

Scripture quotations unless noted otherwise are from the Common English Bible. Copyright © 2011 by the Common English Bible. All rights reserved. Used by permission. www.CommonEnglishBible.com.

Scripture quotations marked NRSVUE are taken from the New Revised Standard Version, Updated Edition. Copyright © 2021 National Council of Churches of Christ in the United States of America. Used by permission. All rights reserved worldwide.

MANUFACTURED IN THE
UNITED STATES OF AMERICA

CONTENTS

CONTENTS

*We are closer to God when we are asking questions
than when we think we have all the answers.*
—Rabbi Abraham Heschel

INTRODUCTION

We learn early in grammar school that the three most common punctuation marks to conclude a sentence are periods, exclamation points, and question marks. Periods are the most common. Most communication is declarative, often a transaction of information. Exclamation points occur occasionally, when there is a need to evoke feeling. Question marks are somewhere in between, less common than periods but more common than exclamation points.

Imagine a life without questions, without curiosity or inquisitiveness. Periods and exclamation points may indicate facts and feelings, but question marks push us forward, into new realms of understanding, reflection, and discovery.

No one knows for sure how the question mark was invented as a part of punctuation, grammar, and human communication. There is an urban legend that the ancient Egyptians first created it based on the look of a cat's tail. An inquisitive cat curls its tail (?) but when it is alarmed, the tail stands straight up (!). There is another theory that the Romans first invented the question mark as a contraction, taking the Latin word *quaestio* and shortening it to *qo* (the first and last letters) as an end marker to every interrogatory sentence. Over time, *qo* was abbreviated to a *q* on top of a dot.[1]

The most widely accepted theory is that the question mark was developed by an eighth-century Englishman named Alcuin of York, whose affinity for reading and writing prompted him to create a symbol to indicate an inflection in the voice at the end of a sentence whenever one asks a question that the listener needs to answer. Try reading or stating questions without that lilt in your voice. It doesn't work. It doesn't command your attention or warrant your response. Alcuin created the question mark to achieve in reading what the lilt does in speech. The question mark alerts the reader and the hearer that they should pay attention, for some response is required of them.

Regardless of how the question mark came to be, we cannot fathom life without the ability to ask or answer questions of one another. A life lived with just declarative and exclamatory sentences would seem two-dimensional. Questions express our openness to new information. It is the capacity to question that enables us to live life most fully. As Rabbi Abraham Heschel said, "We are closer to God when we are asking questions than when we think we have the answers."[2]

> ## The story of your life can be told as a series of pivotal questions.

When you think about it, the story of your life can be told as a series of pivotal questions. Some of the most significant moments of your life have hinged on important questions you had to answer.

What are my values?

How do I present myself to others?

What is my life's purpose?

What gives me contentment?

Who do I trust?

What am I to become?

Every time you answered questions like these, your life took a big step forward.

These are not small questions, and we have all asked them. Often, these hard questions correspond with big changes in our lives that have not just been the most difficult, but also the most necessary. It would be so much easier if life was not so driven by questions and was more driven by declarative, unmistakable statements. If someone would just tell us what to do, if guidance could be as plain as a billboard or as loud as a megaphone, our lives would be simpler.

But questions are how we grow.

We ponder a career change.

We have relationship difficulties.

We contemplate a move.

In these times and many others, we ask questions of ourselves and grow as a result.

Perhaps the most critical and challenging change of all is a theological change, where we question the things that form the bedrock of our faith.

It is no wonder that throughout his ministry, Jesus was quite fond of asking questions. Martin Copenhaver estimates the number of those questions in the self-evident title of his book *Jesus Is the Question: The 307 Questions Jesus Asked and the 3 He Answered*. He said, "Jesus prefers to ask questions rather than to provide direct answers. Jesus chooses to ask a question 307 times in the Gospel accounts. Even if Jesus gives direct answers to as many as 8 questions, that still means that Jesus is almost 40 times more likely to ask a question than he is to give a direct answer."[3]

The questions Jesus asked seem to fall into three basic categories: factual questions, interpretive questions, and evaluative questions.[4] Let's take a look at each category:

Factual

These are the kinds of questions with which we may be most familiar. They request information for which there is a narrow set of acceptable answers. Who, what, when, where, how, how many, and so on. These are the kinds of questions reporters ask when chronicling the facts of an event. Jesus asked questions like these at times.

- "How much bread do you have?" (Matthew 15:34)
- "What is your name?" (Mark 5:9)
- "Who touched me?" (Luke 8:45)

Interpretive

Interpretive questions prompt a person to explore a topic for deeper meaning and greater insight. These are times when Jesus asked his disciples to look below the surface of the obvious and discover a truth they would have otherwise missed.

- "Which is easier—to say, 'Your sins are forgiven,' or to say, 'Get up and walk'?" (Matthew 9:5)
- "Which one of these three was a neighbor to the man who encountered thieves?" (Luke 10:36)
- "If I have told you about earthly things and you don't believe, how will you believe if I tell you about heavenly things?" (John 3:12)

Evaluative

The third category of questions, and the one that narrows the scope of this book, are evaluative questions. These are the ones that summon from us the most personal reflection and response. Rather than factual questions, which can be answered by appealing to quantitative and qualitative information, and interpretive questions, which can be evaluated and debated dispassionately, the most powerful questions Jesus asked are the ones that invite us to go deep into our own minds and hearts for a response. These are the hardest questions to answer, and they are the ones that can be the most transformative.

- *"Who do you say that I am?" (Luke 9:18-20)*
- *"Why are you afraid?" (Matthew 8:23-27)*
- *"Why are you anxious?" (Luke 12:25-31)*
- *"What do you live for?" (Mark 8:34-38)*
- *"Whom will you love?" (Luke 6:27-36)*
- *"What are you looking for?" (John 1:35-38)*

As you read these scripture passages, ponder Jesus's questions for yourself. Allow them to push you, stretch you, and expand the framework through which you come to understand God, yourself, and your relationship with God. Asking and answering questions is how we grow, and these questions Jesus asks of you will be some of the most important ones in your life.

Blessings on your journey.

Questions for Reflection

1. What have been the biggest and toughest questions you have had to answer in your life? How did answering these questions become defining moments for you?

2. How easy or difficult is it for you to ask questions of your own faith? What concerns do you bring to this survey of questions Jesus asks of you?

3. What do you hope emerges from this study for your spiritual life and your commitment to Jesus?

CHAPTER
1

Who Do You Say That I Am?

CHAPTER 1

Who Do You Say That I Am?

Luke 9:18-27

Once when Jesus was praying by himself, the disciples joined him, and he asked them, "Who do the crowds say that I am?"

They answered, "John the Baptist, others Elijah, and still others that one of the ancient prophets has come back to life."

He asked them, "And what about you? **Who do you say that I am?"**

Peter answered, "The Christ sent from God."

Jesus gave them strict orders not to tell this to anyone. He said, "The Human One must suffer many things and be rejected— by the elders, chief priests, and the legal experts—and be killed and be raised on the third day."

Jesus said to everyone, "All who want to come after me must say no to themselves, take up their cross daily, and follow me. All who want to save their lives will lose them. But all who

lose their lives because of me will save them. What advantage
do people have if they gain the whole world for themselves yet
perish or lose their lives? Whoever is ashamed of me and my
words, the Human One will be ashamed of that person when
he comes in his glory and in the glory of the Father and of the
holy angels. I assure you that some standing here won't die
before they see God's kingdom."

(Luke 9:18-27, emphasis added)

Our journey through the questions Jesus asked begins with the most foundational and consequential of them all: "Who do you say that I am?" Your answer to that question determines more than your belief about Jesus; it reveals what you believe about yourself, your relationship to Christ, and your perspective on life.

We find the question in Matthew, Mark, and Luke, and it serves as the pivot point in each of their narratives. Following Peter's answer to the question, and after some additional teaching from Jesus, we read the story of the Transfiguration, which becomes a literary gateway into the second half of Jesus's ministry, leading to Jerusalem and the events of Holy Week.

The events leading up to Jesus's question differ slightly depending on which Gospel you read. In Matthew and Mark, Jesus posed the question as the disciples were passing through the villages near the city of Caesarea Philippi. He had just fed the multitudes with a handful of loaves and fish, been pressed by Pharisees who sought to trap him, and healed a blind man. Jesus and the disciples were now amid the busy crowds near one of the largest cities in the north. Lots of activity, lots of people, lots of noise: that was Matthew and Mark's setting for this question.

Luke tells it a bit differently. In Luke Jesus is all alone. He had just fed the multitudes and then departed for some time to pray. In Luke, the setting is a pause, a breath, a moment of reflection for Jesus and the reader of the Gospel.

Same question, two settings: the busyness of Matthew and Mark, the quiet and stillness of Luke. Both are an occasion for the key question when it comes to our faith: Who do you say that I am?

I suspect that the most consequential, existential questions of life come at one of those two kinds of moments.

We ask deep questions when life is busy and noisy. Amid the hustle and bustle of daily living, with the pressure of deadlines and spinning plates, and fewer hours in a day than are sufficient to check off every item on our to-do lists, we wonder, "Is this all worth it?"

Amid the noise of competing perspectives and the deepening schisms between polarized ideologues, we ponder, "Whose voice should I listen to?"

We ask equally deep questions when life is quiet. In the stillness and dark of late-night insomnia, with eyes wide open and minds racing, we ask ourselves, "What is the meaning of it all?"

In our most honest, authentic prayers, we cry out to God from the deepest parts of our souls, "Who are you? Where are you? And who am I?"

In busyness or stillness, we may ponder the questions that matter the most.

Then, in Luke, Jesus is interrupted. Just as he often was throughout his ministry, his moments of quiet prayer were cut short—like the time he departed to the other side of the lake to pray, or like the time he was asleep in the lower deck of the boat while a storm brewed outside. Here, as he found another rare moment to be by himself, his disciples sought his attention. But this time, he turned the interruption into a chance to ask them a crucial question. When the disciples arrived, Jesus spoke first:

"Who do the crowds say that I am?"

The disciples, who had apparently been keeping their ears to the ground and were in touch with the latest public opinion polls, responded with the most popular answers: John the Baptist, Elijah, one of the ancient prophets come back to life.

> *When we experience something new and awe-inspiring, we use familiar language to get our heads around it.*

Those were all understandable answers. When something novel comes along, we tend to take our impressions of it and squeeze it into the old and familiar. When the internet was new, we described it as the "information superhighway," likening it to a gravel and asphalt road. We adopted the word *email* to liken electronic messages to postal delivery. When the first astronauts traveled into space and sent back pictures of Earth, people used the phrase "big blue marble" to describe what our planet looked like from a distance. When we experience something new and awe-inspiring, we use familiar language to get our heads around it.

Such was the case for this important question that Jesus asked his disciples. Who do the crowds say that I am? *John the Baptist.* Yes, he was like John the Baptist. Jesus was a compelling voice that called people to repentance, action, and a new way of living. But he was more than that. *Elijah*. Yes, he was like Elijah. Jesus was unafraid to challenge those in power and was always ready to aid the poor and vulnerable. But he was much more than that. One of the *ancient prophets*. Yes, he was like the prophets of old, always speaking a message from God, calling people to obedience and surrender. But Jesus was much more than that as well.

As it turns out, that question was just the setup. It was the opening act for what would be the most important question Jesus would ask his disciples—and us:

"And what about you? Who do you say that I am?"

Our journey through the questions of Jesus begins with this, the most significant one of all.

Peter's answer was clear—"The Christ sent from God." *The* Christ, he said. The one foretold by the prophets, the one we have awaited for generations, the one whose arrival had been in motion ever since the fall of Adam and Eve in the garden.

And, the *Christ*. That is, the *Messiah*. Christ, from Greek, and Messiah, from Hebrew, both mean "Anointed One." Jesus is the Anointed One, the Christ, the Messiah. No other person in history had received or deserved this title, and no one would thereafter. Though prophets, priests, and Judah's kings were anointed, the anointed one—the Christ—came to mean in the Second Temple period a figure sent by God, who would usher in God's kingdom. Jesus, Peter says, is that figure. The Christ. Luke is the only Gospel to use the verb form of the word, *chrio*, "to anoint," when Jesus used it in his very first public sermon, in the synagogue, in Luke 4:18-19:

> *The Spirit of the Lord is upon me,*
> > *because the Lord has anointed me.*
> *He has sent me to preach good news to the poor,*
> > *to proclaim release to the prisoners*
> > *and recovery of sight to the blind,*
> > *to liberate the oppressed,*
> > *and to proclaim the year of the Lord's favor.*

For Luke, Jesus is "the Christ" because he has been *anointed* by the "Spirit of the Lord." That is the only qualification and requirement necessary for being the Christ, and it is exclusive to the person of Jesus of Nazareth.

But there is one more thing Peter said. Jesus is not only "the Christ"; he has been "sent from God." He is not simply a human being who transcended into divine status. He is not merely a good teacher who shared holy teaching, or a miracle worker who showcased God's power. He was sent from God, or in other translations, simply, "the Christ of God." In other words, Jesus has a divine origin. He is from God. The early church saw everything Jesus did, wrestled with what it meant, and came to this conclusion: Jesus was one and the same as God. Jesus the Christ was God who had come down to be a human among us. Not just a messenger of God, like John the Baptist, or a spokesperson of God, like Elijah, or a representative of God, like the ancient prophets. When Peter said that Jesus was the Christ sent from God, he expressed the church's first insight into this great mystery.

Jesus was God, anointed by God, sent by God.

In this one verse, in this one question by Jesus and in Peter's clear and direct response, we see the full Trinity on display, long before it would be codified as a doctrine of the church.

Jesus, the Son of God, was sent by God the Father and anointed by God the Spirit.

That, in a nutshell, is the answer to the question, "Who is Jesus?"

So that's it, right? The most important question in the entire Gospels was answered correctly by Peter, and that ought to do it, right? From here, all Peter and the disciples would have to do is share that answer, communicate that message, and the gospel story could be over, and this book that you are reading could end right here. Right?

Not so fast. Because here we discover that the *right* answer is not always the *complete* answer. Especially when it comes to Jesus.

Remember again how Jesus asked the question: "Who do you...*you*...say that I am?"

The question for you and me to answer is not simply, "Who is Jesus?" To use our three-category framework from the introduction, this is more than just a factual question. It is not enough to answer it with doctrinal accuracy or theological clarity. We can answer factual questions correctly, as Peter did. Nor is it simply an interpretive question, inviting us to form opinions about Jesus based on his words and actions and the testimonies of others. To answer it evaluatively—that is, fully and completely—we need to decide what impact the answer will make on our own lives. Anything less is a mere intellectual exercise. And Jesus came to influence much more than just our minds.

This is why Jesus responded to Peter and the disciples the way he did. He did not say, "That's right. Good job, Peter."

Instead, "Jesus gave them strict orders not to tell this to anyone," then taught that he must suffer and die. In essence, Jesus told them, "OK. I am the Christ sent from God. But there's more to it than that. In fact, don't say a word to anyone about your answer to my question, because it is incomplete. It's only partially right. It's a good start, but there's more to know."

Here is exactly what he said in response: "The Human One must suffer many things and be rejected—by the elders, chief priests, and the legal experts—and be killed and be raised on the third day."

Then, in verses 23-27, he drilled down on the specifics of what this would mean for them.

> *"All who want to come after me must say no to themselves, take up their cross daily, and follow me. All who want to save their lives will lose them. But all who lose their lives because of me will save them. What advantage do people have if they gain the whole world for themselves yet perish or lose their lives? Whoever is ashamed of me and my words, the Human One will be ashamed of that person when he comes in his glory and in the glory of the Father and of the holy angels. I assure you that some standing here won't die before they see God's kingdom."*

If you really believe that Jesus is "the Christ of God," then everything in your life ought to change. You need to say no to yourself, take up the cross, and follow Jesus. You need to lose your life in order to save it. Gaining the whole world or saving your reputation no longer matters. The only thing that matters is orienting your entire life toward living out the kingdom of God.

As it turns out, the Gospels have a lot more to tell us about how best to answer the question, "Who do you say that I am?"

In fact, it would be helpful to think about that question in a few slightly different ways to get a fuller picture of what Jesus was really asking and how we might best answer it.

Here are the three questions we will explore for the balance of this chapter:

1. Who do you say Jesus is ... every day?
2. Who do you say Jesus is now?
3. What difference does your answer make in your life?

The Journey Is Part of the Answer

If all that mattered was answering Jesus's question correctly one time, then Peter had it made. He aced the test. He would have graduated into full discipleship. But there was much more that he had to discover. It's one thing to demonstrate what one knows about Jesus. It is quite another to discover who one is in relation to that Jesus every day. That matter requires regular, daily examination over a lifetime of exploration. It can even expand and change over time.

In his *Directions for Renewing Our Covenant with God*, John Wesley offered five steps toward faithful living in Christ. His fourth step was:

> Fourthly, resolve to be faithful. Having engaged your hearts, opened your mouths, and subscribed with your hands to the Lord, resolve in his strength never to go back.[1]

11

Wesley recognized that each day is filled with fresh temptations to renounce one's commitments to Jesus, succumb to spiritual apathy and lethargy, and return to one's sinful ways. He called people to "resolve" to never to go back.

That word *resolve* comes from the Latin root *solvere*, which means "to loosen." Adding the prefix *re-* creates *resolvere*, which means "to unloose or dissolve."

To resolve to be faithful means to loosen, dissolve, and dismantle all that would pull us back into sin, away from our primary commitment to Jesus Christ. For Wesley, that act of resolution is a regular calling over the course of one's lifetime. A lapse of attentiveness can be costly.

Years ago, my older daughter, Grace, was eager to earn her learner's permit to drive. For weeks, she studied the manual and prepared for the test, looking forward to passing that milestone moment in her maturity.

She aced the written test, beamed for her photograph on the permit, and swelled with pride over her accomplishment. As we walked out of the motor vehicle office, she said to me, "Dad, can I drive us home?"

Now, all of her knowledge about driving until that point had been book knowledge. She had not been in the driver's seat and had never taken the wheel. During that first driving tutorial, she did great. She handled the car beautifully, made smooth turns around the neighborhood, and pulled in and out of parking spots.

After ninety minutes of driving, I told her, "You've done really well, Grace. Great job. Let's go home now."

She saw a big parking lot nearby and said, "OK, Dad. But can we practice parking, just one more time for the day?"

"Sure," I said. She pulled into the spot, right between the yellow lines…and made a mistake. For just a brief moment…just for a second, her mind drifted a bit, and she forgot the difference between the brake and gas pedals. She slammed down on the gas pedal, thinking the car would slow down, but instead we hopped the parking stop, onto the median, and slammed into a light post.

I looked at her. She was stunned. I calmly said, "I'll drive us home now."

Grace learned the hard way that simply getting the textbook answers correct in a single moment in time is not enough to become a responsible driver. It requires regular focus and diligence. (I'm happy to say that as of this writing, she has not been in a car accident since.)

> *The grace of God not only meets us where we are; it also guides us into becoming what we are intended to be.*

The good news is that the grace of God not only meets us where we are; it also guides us into becoming what we are intended to be. It helps us profess our faith, and then live out our faith, with the kind of daily resolve that will enable us to stay focused on and attentive to Jesus.

Allowing Our Relationships to Change

The passage of time adds another dimension to the life of faith. It not only necessitates regular resolve; it invites expansion and adaptation.

Think about human relationships, especially with someone you have known for a very long time. It may be a spouse, a partner, or a lifelong friend. When you were first getting to know that person, there were feelings of frequent discovery. Everything felt new in your relationship, as you were finding out about each other's personalities and passions, as well as your shared interests and aspirations. Think about the conversations you had when you were first getting to know each other, and what they revealed about the other person and yourself. You had to learn who that person was, which in part meant learning who he or she was not.

Inevitably, over time, relationships change, don't they? Events occur that push you to see each other in new ways; sometimes they challenge what you thought you knew about a person, and sometimes they confirm your assumptions. If that person were to ask you, "Who do you say that I am?" at various points in your relationship, your responses would have strong consistency over time. But they would also have various degrees of nuance, depth, and maturity as you go through life together.

No relationship is static, and neither is our perception of our relationships. That is certainly the case with our relationship with Jesus.

In his book *Let Ministry Teach: A Guide for Theological Reflection*, Robert Kinast offers three paradigms, or models, for examining the relationship between our theology and our life experience, between what we believe about God and how we expect God to be active in our lives.

Imagine two circles. The first circle represents your theology, which encompasses your collection of convictions and perceptions of who God is. The second circle represents some significant event that has occurred in your life that is prompting you to ask about God's presence and activity within it.

Now imagine superimposing those two circles, one on top of the other.

The first paradigm, by far the easiest and most comforting, is that the two circles are perfectly congruent with each other. Your experience resonates with your belief, and your belief interprets your experience. Everything makes sense.

It is likely that throughout your life, there has rarely been such perfect congruity between those two circles. The circles have not exactly fit; there has been tension between the two. These moments are rich with possibility for critical theological reflection.

So, imagine a second paradigm, where the circle of our theology is wider than the circle of a particular life experience. To find congruity, our theology pushes us to expand our perception of what was happening in that event. Might God have been present in a way we weren't noticing at first? Was God summoning something of me that I was not willing to acknowledge? Is God pushing me to repentance or surrender? Is there a way to enlarge my view of that event to acknowledge and affirm God's presence and activity?

These are not easy tensions to navigate. After Peter answered Jesus's question, for the remainder of Luke's gospel and well into the Book of Acts, Peter would be challenged to expand his interpretation of life events to see and accept what Jesus was summoning of him.

But there is a third paradigm. Imagine times when the circle of life's experience is *larger* than your circle of *theology*. Imagine what happens when that which has happened is bigger than the theological answers at your disposal. To find congruity, it is our understanding of God that needs to expand in order to make sense of our life experience. Experience teaches us sometimes who God is not, showing us that we have conceived God too narrowly. This is not to suggest that we should veer away from what is central or essential to the faith. Instead, it is to make our faith a living one, allowing it to breathe, expand, and adapt to a wider set of challenges that life brings us. It is not to say experience dictates orthodoxy. It is to say that God can use our experiences to open our eyes to deeper, richer ways to see Jesus, and renew our faith in him.[2]

I will return to the image of these three circles and relate my own personal story to them in the final chapter. For now, I will say only that these kinds of tensions are critical moments in our faith, as they push us—sometimes painfully—to let go of constrictive images of God and exchange them for healthier, more robust ways to see God.

There is a scene in the 2006 the film *Talladega Nights: The Ballad of Ricky Bobby* that humorously depicts (and exaggerates) our propensity to see God strictly on our own terms. It is at the family dinner table of NASCAR driver and lead character Ricky Bobby, played by Will Ferrell. He is surrounded by his wife and children, his father-in-law, and his best friend, Cal. Ricky begins to offer grace at the dinner table with these words: "Dear Lord Baby Jesus . . ." As he continues the prayer, he keeps repeating versions of "Dear Baby Jesus" or "dear tiny, infant Jesus . . ."

Ricky's wife, Carly, interrupts: "Hey, um, you know, sweetie, Jesus did grow up. You don't always have to call him baby. It's a bit odd and off-putting to pray to a baby."

Ricky responds, "Well, look, I like the Christmas Jesus best, and I'm saying grace. When you say grace, you can say it to "Grown Up Jesus," or "Teenage Jesus," or "Bearded Jesus," or whoever you want."

Eventually Ricky's friend Cal pipes in: "I like to picture Jesus in a tuxedo T-shirt, because it says, like, 'I want to be formal, but I'm here to party, too.' 'Cause I like to party, so I like my Jesus to party."

And one of Ricky's little boys says, "I like to picture Jesus as a ninja, fightin' off evil samurai."

And Ricky concludes: "Okay. Dear eight-pound, six-ounce, newborn, infant Jesus—don't even know a word yet. Just a little infant, so cuddly, but still omnipotent—we just thank you for all the races I've won and the $21.2 million…that I have accrued over this past season…Thank you for all your power and grace, dear baby God. Amen."[3]

Every time I have used this illustration in a sermon, people in the congregation have laughed because of the inanity of such a prayer. But when you think about it, deep down inside, Ricky Bobby's theology is a common starting point for us. We expect our view of God to fit our life experiences, our agendas, and our perspectives. We want to picture and to pray to whichever Jesus we like best.

When one of life's inevitable curveballs comes our way—moments of loss, grief, suffering—that circle of theology feels inadequate to rise to the challenge of the moment, and we are left struggling.

It is in those moments when Jesus asks us, "Who do you say that I am...*now?*"

Those can be profound moments of growth and new understanding in our spiritual lives. It is not that the question requires a different answer than the one Peter gave. Jesus is still, and always will be, the Messiah of God. But it is our understanding of what that answer means and how it impacts us that we must allow to flex, breathe, and adapt to our ever-changing lives.

Expanding Our Theology of Prayer

I have often experienced the need to nuance my theology when it comes to my prayer life. There are times when I have gone through a drought in my practice of prayer. Maybe you have too. These are seasons when we struggle with how to pray, what to say, when to pray, and most critically, why to pray.

In those moments, I have learned to ask myself, and those who have come to me with similar needs, "Who is this God you are praying to? What is the image you have of this God to whom you are praying?" Jesus would ask it this way: "Who do you say that I am?"

In the early days of my relationship with Jesus, I pictured him as a strong, tall man who sits high and mighty on a throne up in heaven. There are lots of biblical references that support such an image, and it was how I pictured him when I was new in the faith. That image framed what I thought prayer was: I needed to speak to such royalty with formal language and proper address. But when those words escaped me, or when the circumstances of life rendered those words meaningless, I entered a prayer drought. That drought became an invitation to expand my circle of theology, my view of Jesus.

There have been times, I must admit, when my view of Jesus was the equivalent of a cosmic vending machine, or a giant butler: Jesus was there primarily to grant me what I needed so long as I punched the right buttons, deposited the right amount of spiritual currency, and waited long enough for the blessing to drop. You and I well know that such prayers don't always bring the results we are looking for. So, again, I entered a prayer drought, and it became an invitation for me to expand my circle of theology, my view of who I said Jesus was.

Then, of course, there is the image of Jesus as a friend, sitting in the room next to me, with whom I can talk face-to-face, eye to eye. That image is also rooted in the Bible, and it has brought me and others great comfort over the years. But then there have been moments—and you may have experienced them too—when it seemed as if my friend was not talking back. Even today, the friend seems absent sometimes, or even to be looking the other way. Jesus himself went through that crisis when he cried out, "My God, my God, why have you forsaken me?" (Matthew 27:46 NRSVUE). Those prayer droughts feel like the hardest, most crushing of all. But they can also provide the most accelerated, most urgent expansion in our view of Jesus.

As our relationship with Jesus changes, it is allowed, and even encouraged, to change, adapt, and mature. We must always see him as the "Messiah of God." But we can also expand our theology, and with it our corresponding spiritual practices, like Scripture reading, fasting, tithing, witnessing, and most certainly, prayer.

The journey through my own prayer droughts has led me to a view of God that has sustained me a great deal over time. It is one in which God is present in all things, embedded in every moment, as close as my own breath (the Hebrew word for *spirit* and *breath* are the same, after all). This has enabled me to see prayer as more of an attentiveness of heart, mind, and spirit, in which my every breath can become a prayer to God. Every chew of food, every gasp of delight, every splash of water as I bathe, every heartbeat I feel, can become a moment of prayer and delight and joy as I learn to sense the presence of God within me.

These kinds of recognitions can come when we learn to hear Jesus asking us, "Who do you say that I am... right now?"

What Difference Does It Make?

The last nuance of Jesus's question may be the most important one of all. How should your understanding of who Jesus is make any difference in your life?

It is a question whose consequences are far beyond mere individual impact. We remember that the same Christian religion that formed Mother Teresa and Billy Graham also reared Adolf Hitler. The same Christian church that has built hospitals, schools, and social services around the world also brought the Inquisition, the Crusades, and the persecution of some of our greatest thinkers through history.

Yes, it is important to answer the question correctly: Who do you say that I am? The Messiah of God. But it is also important to answer it justly: What difference should that make in how we live and act in the world?

The late Peter Gomes, author and professor at Harvard Divinity School, wrote a marvelous book called *The Scandalous Gospel of Jesus: What's So Good about the Good News?* In it he said,

> The question should not be "What would Jesus do?" but rather, more dangerously, "What would Jesus have me do?" The onus is not on Jesus but on us, for Jesus did not come to ask semidivine human beings to do impossible things. He came to ask human beings to live up to their full humanity; he wants us to live in the full implication of our human gifts, and that is far more demanding.[4]

To say that Jesus is the Messiah of God is therefore to willfully follow the life and example that Jesus gives us, and to love as God loves. It is to be governed by a heart of generosity, empathy, and compassion toward others. It is to take the principles of the Sermon on the Mount—as difficult and even irrational as they may seem—and adopt them as a guide for living and relating to others. It is to seek the way of peace over violence, and to seek the expansion of God's hospitality to those who feel rejected, shunned, ignored, and even harmed by past experiences with the church.

To say that Jesus is the Messiah of God is therefore to willfully follow the life and example that Jesus gives us, and to love as God loves.

We do this so that others can hear Jesus ask them the same question, "Who do you say that I am," answer it for themselves, and discover the life that God has always intended for them.

Not long ago I received an email from someone whose story simply blew me away. At the start of the global COVID-19 pandemic, we moved our worship services at Hyde Park UMC to an online platform, as many congregations did. It has been a learning curve from the very beginning, but it has expanded the reach of God's love to a wider network of people around the world than we've ever had before.

That includes this person, a newcomer who discovered our church online, whom I will call Rodney. He shared with me the amazing work that God had been doing in his life. This is what he wrote me:

> I came across Hyde Park UMC's "Making God's Love Real" recordings in a very intense search for meaning in the early months of 2020. I've been a very tough atheist for most of my life, but I've also dealt with very strong feelings of depression and anxiety for as long as I can remember, which have made me somewhat of a nihilist. 2019 was really damaging for me, but last year was full of healing and progress, in which you and HPUMC played a very big role.
>
> I now consider myself a Christian and know I will make it through my hardest patches in the future thanks to the faith you sparked in me, as I've done this year. But I also still think rationality and science are the way to solve most problems in this

world, therapy and medication are very powerful tools, and inequality across racial, cultural, and gender lines is real. And the reason I can now break this apparent dichotomy is the listening of your teachings.

You do a great service to this world by helping articulate the complementary nature of science and religion with such a humane approach. I remain forever thankful to you and Hyde Park United Methodist Church, and hope someday I can give back at least a fraction of the love I've received thanks to your worship services.

I have had numerous conversations with Rodney ever since that first email exchange. He has since told me that he hasn't missed a single service with us online, and that he is now getting involved in a local faith community near where he lives.

This is the difference Jesus can make when we offer ourselves fully to him. He can transform our hearts and shape our behavior. He can align our priorities with God's best intentions for the world. He can offer peace and hope when we are suffering and struggling. And he can guide us as a people of God toward acts of compassion, healing, and love, rather than violence, cruelty, and hatred.

He is the Messiah of God, in us, through us, and for the world.

Questions for Reflection

1. When do you remember first pondering the question of who Jesus is to you?

2. When have there been times when your circle of life experience has matched up perfectly with the circle of your theology?

3. When has there been tension between those two circles? In what ways did those tensions push you to grow and see both yourself and God in a more nuanced, mature way?

CHAPTER 2

Why Are You Afraid?

CHAPTER

2

CHAPTER 2

Why Are You Afraid?

Matthew 8:23-27

When Jesus got into a boat, his disciples followed him. A huge storm arose on the lake so that waves were sloshing over the boat. But Jesus was asleep. They came and woke him, saying, "Lord, rescue us! We're going to drown!"

*He said to them, "**Why are you afraid, you people of weak faith?**" Then he got up and gave orders to the winds and the lake, and there was a great calm.*

The people were amazed and said, "What kind of person is this? Even the winds and the lake obey him!"

(Matthew 8:23-27)

***

Lord, purge our eyes to see
Within the seed a tree
Within the glowing egg a bird,
Within the shroud a butterfly:

Till taught by such, we see
Beyond all creatures Thee,
And hearken for Thy tender word,
And hear it, "Fear not: it is I."
　　　—*Christina Rossetti*,
　　　"Judge Not According to the Appearance"[1]

It should be no surprise that one of Jesus's questions to his disciples was, "Why are you afraid?" Fear is a lingering presence in the human experience, and Scripture is no exception. The command not to be afraid occurs dozens of times throughout the Bible. (One popular notion is that it occurs 365 times. That number seems like an interpretive stretch but nonetheless reminds us that overcoming fear is a daily task.)

Fear is one of the most prevalent and haunting human emotions. We have all experienced fear to some degree at various stages in our lives. It doesn't help that we live in a culture that thrives on reminding us just how much there is to be afraid of. A recent documentary called *Thrive* describes how entire cottage industries have been developed to keep you in a constant state of panic. Some politicians would have you believe there is danger lurking beyond every horizon, and you had best elect them if you want to be safe. Consultants want you to hire them to keep your business from going south. And, sad to say, there are even preachers who would try to convince you that evil is just around the corner, so you'd better come to church and drop your check in the offering plate.

There is fear all around us, and we've been conditioned to believe it even when it's irrational.

I'm reminded of the humorous story of a pharmacist who was being reprimanded by his boss for constantly screwing up prescriptions. He told him that if he messed up one more medication, he was fired.

The next day an old man walked in with an embarrassingly persistent cough. He could barely talk to the pharmacist and give him the prescription for cough syrup from his doctor without launching into a coughing fit. The pharmacist, nervous about making sure he got the medicine right, fumbled through his bottles and jars and filled the man's prescription.

Moments after the man walked out of the drugstore, the boss went behind the counter to check up on the pharmacist.

"Good grief, man!" the boss said. "Why in the world didn't you give the man his cough syrup? You gave him a laxative instead! Give me one good reason why I shouldn't fire you!"

"Well," the pharmacist said, "follow me." He led the boss to the front window of the store, and they looked outside just as the man had taken his medicine. He was leaning up against a light post. And he wasn't coughing.

"See that?" the pharmacist said. "Now he's too afraid to cough!"

We are prone to believe that there are reasons to be afraid all around us. It should not be a surprise that Jesus addresses fear directly.

Nor should we be surprised that he does so in the context of a stormy sea. Throughout the Hebrew Bible, as in many other ancient Near Eastern texts, the sea is a symbol of chaos and death. It's a force that inspires fear.

In Genesis, a flood wiped creation off the planet. In the Exodus, a large body of water stood in the way of the Israelites' escape from slavery into freedom. In Joshua, the waters prevented the people from moving from their wilderness wandering into the hope of the Promised Land. In the Psalms and the Prophets, the sea is described as the dwelling place of mythical beasts called Rahab and Leviathan, embodiments of all that is menacing and fearful in the world.

> *An overwhelming sense of fear can feel like drowning, flailing, and sinking into forces that appear beyond our control.*

Often, when the Bible wants to describe fear, it plunges you deep into its depths. An overwhelming sense of fear can feel like drowning, flailing, and sinking into forces that appear beyond our control.

It is no wonder that among the questions Jesus asked, we find an acknowledgment of our fears in the context of a storm-tossed sea.

Matthew's Version of the Calming of the Seas

The stilling of the storm by Jesus is so well-known that Matthew, Mark, and Luke all record it. Matthew even has two variations of it: here in Matthew 8, and another in chapter 14.

In each version, there is a similar plot. The disciples are on a boat on the storm-prone Sea of Galilee. The wind and waves escalate to the point of sheer terror, and fear grips the disciples. We can imagine ourselves in their places, frantically bailing with our buckets, plugging holes and sealing fissures, only to see the ship (and our lives) cracking at the seams. We know what it is to be flailing, drowning, treading water through life. This is what the disciples felt. This is what we feel.

It is then that the disciples had the presence of mind to summon Jesus. We all know what he did. He spoke into the wind and calmed the storm in an instant, leaving a band of soaking, drippy disciples in jaw-dropped disbelief.

Again, the story is repeated throughout the Synoptic Gospels, with two versions in Matthew alone. What is fascinating to me about this rendition of the story in Matthew 8 is what Jesus does *before* he speaks to the storm. He first speaks to the disciples. They awake him from his slumber, and they are both panicked and angry. *"Lord, rescue us! We're going to drown!"* That's when Jesus decides first to speak, not to the storm, but to them:

"Why are you afraid, you people of weak faith?"

At first glance, this seems like an odd and ill-timed question, doesn't it? Wouldn't it have made more sense for Jesus to utter something declarative, such as "Calm down"? Or even something exclamatory, like, "Have more faith!" If we had been the disciples, wouldn't we have thought to ourselves, *You know, Jesus, we'll be happy to entertain all the questions and listen to all the lectures you want to give us. But could you maybe, pretty please, take care of the storm first?*

I'll admit that when I read that question, "Why are you afraid, you people of weak faith?" I cannot help but hear a tone of rebuke and even disappointment from Jesus in that moment. "Hey, disciples, what is wrong with you? How could you be afraid when I'm here? What don't you all get?"

What if Jesus asked the question differently than I usually imagine? How would hearing his words in a different tone change our interpretation of the question? As we've discovered in an era of email, text messaging, and social media, we cannot assume a person's tone simply by reading his or her words. It would have been so much nicer if we could have seen a video of Jesus asking that question.

Asking and Hearing the Question Differently

Leadership and communications expert Sharon Ellison wrote a book titled *Taking the War Out of Our Words: The Art of Powerful Non-Defensive Communication*. She reminds us that body language, gestures, and tone of voice mean everything when we are speaking to each other in a tense situation. She gives as an example this question: "Are you upset about something?"

Imagine if I were to ask you that question in a stern, interrogational kind of way: "ARE YOU UPSET ABOUT SOMETHING?" You would detect in my face, body, and tone a kind of interrogation that would easily escalate the tension of the moment. Even if that were not my intent, that is what I would be communicating, even subconsciously, through the way I posed the question.

That is how we might first hear Jesus's question, "Why are you afraid, you people of weak faith?" But since we have no video recording of Jesus asking it, what if the Spirit were inviting us to hear his question with a different intent altogether—not to escalate the tension for the disciples in that moment, but to offer a glimpse of peace and even hope?

In her book Ellison ponders how different it would be to hear the question with a quieter, more inquisitive tone. Try reading it that way to yourself: "Are you upset about something?" Asked that way, the question is less about accusing or judging and more about empathy and curiosity. Elsewhere, Ellison notes that when you look up the word *question* in a dictionary, the definition most often includes the word *interrogation* and rarely includes the word *curiosity*.[2]

What if the question that Jesus would ask the disciples, and ask us today, is less about interrogation and more about curiosity? Not "Why are you afraid, *you people of weak faith?*" but, "Why *are* you afraid? Why *is* your faith little?"

I love this idea that a simple question asked with earnest curiosity might actually de-escalate tension in the moment. I once heard someone ask Richard Rohr what he would do if, in a social gathering, someone were to utter something rude and ideologically opposite of his own perspective. Would he just ignore it to preserve the peace and comfort of everyone around them, or would he strongly rebut the rude comment with his own opinion? Rohr responded, "I would probably say something clearly but calmly, like, 'Hmm. That's not the way I see it,' and leave it at that."

That kind of response neither escalates or avoids the tension, but calmly enters into it by introducing novelty and curiosity. It may lead to more conversation, or it may at least plant the seed in that other person's mind that there are other ways to see the question.

I wonder if that is what is happening here, in this storm-tossed boat on the Sea of Galilee. Maybe Jesus is neither ignoring the disciples' fear nor rebuking them for it, but introducing a way to conquer their fear through the simple act of asking a question with disarming curiosity.

"Why *are* you afraid? What is it that scares you? What do you think is the limit of your faith right now?"

What would it be like to hear Jesus asking you those questions right now, for whatever areas of fear you are facing today? Imagine Jesus asking you these questions, not to accuse you of not having enough faith, but to invite you to explore the source of that fear, to test its validity, and to learn to rely on what is true instead of on the falsehoods that fear would have you believe.

Wise Buddhist author and spiritual guide Pema Chödrön tells a fable about a young warrior whose teacher ordered her to go into battle against fear. She didn't want to do that. She told her teacher that "it seemed too aggressive; it was scary; it seemed unfriendly." But the teacher said she must, then instructed her for the battle.

"The day arrived. The student warrior stood on one side, and fear stood on the other. The warrior was feeling very small, and fear was looking big and wrathful. They both had their weapons. The young warrior roused herself and went toward fear." Instead of striking at it or waiting for it to strike, the young warrior bowed three times and then began to question her opponent.

She asked "'May I have permission to go into battle with you?' Fear said, 'Thank you for showing me so much respect that you ask permission.' Then the young warrior said: 'How can I defeat you?' Fear replied, 'My weapons are that I talk fast, and I get very close to your face. Then you get completely unnerved, and you do whatever I say. If you don't do what I tell you, I have no power. You can listen to me, and you can have respect for me…But if you don't do what I say, I have no power."'

"In that way," says Chödrön, "the student warrior learned how to defeat fear."[3]

What are you afraid of? Chances are you are afraid of something. There are valid and plentiful reasons for us to feel fear. I suspect that whatever the source of your fear is today, you are not alone. It does not take much of a trigger for that fear to escalate the tension you are feeling within yourself. You can take heart that Jesus comes to you right now, not to raise that tension even further, but to teach you how to de-escalate that tension by inviting you to ask simple questions of yourself and of your fears.

Look fear in the eye and ask, "Where did you come from?"

Stand firm right now. Look fear in the eye and ask, "Where did you come from?" What is the early memory that is so etched into your mind that you have a recurring recording in your mind that makes you afraid?

The question you ask yourself might be, "Do I believe that my fear is the truth?" I've heard that we can think of FEAR as an acronym for False Evidence Appearing Real. The young warrior within you has a choice not to believe the falsehoods that fear would have you believe. A recent study by the Department of Psychology at the University of Pennsylvania concluded that 91 percent of the things we worry about do not actually come true.[4]

Which leads to the next question we might ask when it comes to fear: "What is the worst that could happen?" I know many of us are very good at spinning out worst-case scenarios for the fears we are facing. But as you do, remember that no matter what happens, God will give you what you need to face it, come what may. God has done it before and will do it again.

This is the lesson the disciples needed to learn in the boat that day. Even if the worst thing were to happen—the boat crashes to pieces and the disciples are left treading water—they would realize in that moment that Jesus was with them. The God who parted the waves in the Red Sea, saved the ark from the floodwaters, and tamed the watery beast Leviathan in Job—that God would still be with them.

A Lesson from John Wesley

In September 2017, my city of Tampa, Florida, was in the prospective path of a dangerous hurricane named Irma. It was scheduled to take a northward turn over the early hours of Sunday morning and hit us directly later that afternoon. We made the decision as a church to cancel in-person worship that day as parishioners frantically hunkered down, secured their belongings, and in many cases evacuated to safer ground hundreds of miles away.

During our normal worship time, I appeared live on our church's social media page to offer a pseudoworship experience and a message of comfort to all of us who were experiencing such fear. I began with these words:

> This has been quite a week. Hurricane Irma has been a looming threat for the past several days and is now still on the verge of making landfall.

For many of us, our nerves are frazzled and our minds are on high alert. Emotions have vacillated between fear for the future and a determination to press on. These have been tiring days and sleepless nights, watching the latest track updates, waiting in lines for water and gas, and running through exhausting mental checklists. Many of us have been on edge, filled with worry, anticipating the worst.

I then shared the story of Jesus calming the storm in Mark's Gospel, whose vivid description of the conditions feels like a page from a Hollywood film script.

"Gale-force winds arose, and waves crashed against the boat so that the boat was swamped" (Mark 4:37).

Mark described the weather conditions and the disciples' fear in a way that accurately reflected our own fearful experience as Hurricane Irma drew near. Just as the disciples were bailing water and plugging leaks, we were filling sandbags, standing in lines for water, waiting in lines for gas. And then, Mark suddenly shifts our attention from the storm and gives us an inside peek into what's happening inside the boat, in the stern, in the sleeping quarters.

There we find the Son of God, sleeping on a cushion.

We have come to learn many things about Jesus Christ. We know he was a stunning teacher. He was a miracle worker, a compassionate person. But now, add to the list of Jesus's qualities that he was a heavy sleeper! In a moment of fear and anxiety, Jesus located within himself a center of peace and calm amid the storm.

How did he do it? How was he able to have, as Paul described it in Philippians, a peace "that exceeds all understanding" (4:7)? How can we have such peace? Might it have something to do with the knowledge that no matter what, God is in this with us?

During my message as we awaited Irma, I shared this story from the life of John Wesley, who early in his life was in a hurricane on the sea. He didn't call it that, but based on his description of being in a storm-tossed ship in the middle of the Atlantic, it sure sounded like one:

> At noon our third storm began. At four it was more violent than before...The winds roared round about us, and (what I have never heard before) whistled as distinctly as if it had been a human voice. The ship not only rocked to and fro with the utmost violence, but shook and jarred with so unequal, grating a motion, that one could not but with great difficulty keep hold on any thing, nor stand a moment without it. Every ten minutes came a shock against the stern or side of the ship, which one would think should dash the planks in pieces.[5]

Sounds like scary stuff. It's enough to make us fear for the worst, and there was a part of Wesley that certainly did. Yet, amid the storm, Wesley found solace in a surprising source. Among his shipmates was a group of German Moravian Christians whose calm, peaceful strength made an indelible impression on him. This is what he wrote in his journal:

> In the midst of the psalm wherewith their service began, the sea broke over, split the main sail in pieces, covered the ship, and poured in between

the decks, as if the great deep had already swallowed us up. A terrible screaming began among the English. The Germans calmly sung on. I asked one of them afterwards, "Were you not afraid?" He answered, "I thank God, No." I asked, "But were not your women and children afraid?" He replied mildly, "No; our women and children are not afraid to die."

From them I went to their crying, trembling neighbours, and pointed out to them the difference in the hour of trial, between him that feareth God, and him that feareth him not. At twelve the wind fell. This was the most glorious day which I have hitherto seen.[6]

The countenance of these Moravian Christians made a deep impact on Wesley's life. It not only kept him calm during the storm, but it inspired him to draw closer to God in his walk with Christ. Here he was, a minister of the gospel, a spiritual leader of people, and a missionary to a foreign land. But even he had fears. He needed the example of a humble, centered, calm people to remind him that God was in this.

What can we learn from a sleeping Jesus and a singing group of Moravians? God is with us.

I asked people joining me on social media, as we prepared for Hurricane Irma, wherever they were, in the midst of whatever they were doing, to stop and sing a familiar hymn born out of the fear and tragedy on a storm-tossed sea:

When peace, like a river, attendeth my way, when sorrows like sea billows roll;

whatever my lot, thou hast taught me to say, It is well, it is well with my soul.[7]

I then asked them to join me in singing a stanza of "Be Still, My Soul:"

> Be still, my soul: your God will undertake
> to guide the future, as in ages past.
> Your hope, your confidence let nothing shake;
> all now mysterious shall be bright at last.
> Be still, my soul: the waves and winds still know
> the Christ who ruled them while he dwelt below.[8]

There's one more important part of this story with the Moravians. On that ship, they not only sang; they also served others. They did the jobs to help other people on board that no one else would do. They took it upon themselves to make others' lives better. This deeply impacted Wesley as well, as he reflected in his journal:

> Of their humility they had given a continual proof, by performing those servile offices for the other passengers, which none of the English would undertake; for which they desired, and would receive no pay, saying, "it was good for their proud hearts," and "their loving Saviour had done more for them." And every day had given them occasion of showing a meekness which no injury could move. If they were pushed, struck, or thrown down, they rose again and went away; but no complaint was found in their mouth.[9]

I told the congregation that no matter what happened with the storm that was headed our way, and no matter what the devastation and aftermath that could follow, there were two tasks that God was calling us to perform: to sing and to serve. The first brings comfort to us in our fears, and the second brings comfort to others through us. I invited them to do both over the coming hours and days, because it is good to be the church in moments like this.

In the midst of our fears, God is always calling us to sing and to serve. We are to receive the comfort of God within us and to share the comfort of God with those around us.

> *We are to receive the comfort of God within us and to share the comfort of God with those around us.*

What Kind of Man Is This?

As it turns out, our story from the Gospels is about Jesus calming two storms, not just one. He calms the physical storms *around* us, the wind and the waves of our circumstances. But even before that, he speaks to the storm *within* us, to show us how to combat our stormy fears through the simple act of asking it questions:

Where does your fear come from? Do you believe that your fear is the truth? What is the worst that could happen? What would you be able to do if you weren't afraid?

There is one more question. It's the one that serves as the coda to both Matthew's and Luke's versions of the story. After

41

Jesus rebuked the storm, and the disciples were dripping wet with astonishment and marvel, the story ends with a question, not from Jesus, but from within themselves.

The disciples asked, "What sort of man is this, that even the winds and the sea obey him?" (Matthew 8:27 NRSVUE; see also Luke 8:25).

This is the Gospel writers' way of asking, "Now, where have we seen this before?" Who does Jesus remind you of? The answer, of course, is the power that Jesus demonstrated on the Sea of Galilee is the same power that God has displayed all throughout the Bible in the face of fear.

God does not leave us to be overcome by our fears. God comes to us through Jesus Christ, conquering the waves of our apprehensions, stilling the storms of uncertainty. In Jesus God calls us to trust and surrender ourselves to the loving and powerful arms of God.

That is the future that God desires for you. It is a life that is neither free from fear nor dictated by it. It's a life in which you engage your fear and allow God to transform it to make you stronger and more faithful.

Questions for Reflection

1. In what ways is your life driven by too much fear? To what degree do you believe those fears are the truth?

2. What difference does it make for you to hear Jesus ask this question more out of curiosity than of judgment?

3. How will you allow God to help you address your fears rather than avoid them or be dictated by them?

CHAPTER
3

Why
Are You
Anxious?

CHAPTER 3

Why Are You Anxious?

Luke 12:25-31

"Who among you by worrying can add a single moment to your life? If you can't do such a small thing, why worry about the rest? Notice how the lilies grow. They don't wear themselves out with work, and they don't spin cloth. But I say to you that even Solomon in all his splendor wasn't dressed like one of these. If God dresses grass in the field so beautifully, even though it's alive today and tomorrow it's thrown into the furnace, how much more will God do for you, you people of weak faith! Don't chase after what you will eat and what you will drink. Stop worrying. All the nations of the world long for these things. Your Father knows that you need them. Instead, desire his kingdom and these things will be given to you as well."

(Luke 12:25-31, emphasis added)

If we imagine a list of Gospel passages titled "Easier Said Than Done," this pair of questions from Jesus in Luke 12 would likely be near the top: "Who among you by worrying can add a single moment to your life? If you can't do such a small thing, why worry about the rest?"

We wouldn't be alone in thinking that way. Just think about all the anxious people who encountered Jesus in the Gospels.

"Jesus, my son is possessed by a demon. Please heal him."

"Jesus, this storm is about to kill us. Please wake up."

"Jesus, I'd like to be your right-hand man. Please promote me."

"Jesus, the people are hungry. Please feed them."

In some ways, Jesus's ministry can feel like one long, waiting line of people seeking relief for their worry and anxiety.

If we're being honest, aren't you and I in that line too?

"Jesus, I really don't know what I'm supposed to do with my life. Please tell me."

"Jesus, I wish I could get over this grief over my loved one's death. Please comfort me."

"Jesus, I feel so lonely after my divorce. Please encourage me."

"Jesus, I feel so helpless after the doctor's diagnosis. Please give me hope."

So, when Jesus asked his disciples, and asks us, in so many words, "Why are you so anxious?" there is a part of us that wants to reply, "Well, who *isn't* anxious?"

Jesus's question is a bit of a paradox, if you think about it. On the one hand, it often comes to us at just the right time, speaking right into the heart of the worries and anxieties we carry in the moment, providing just the right dose of comfort.

Jesus's references to lilies that don't toil (verses 27–28) and sparrows that don't stress (verses 6–7) are like a warm blanket to our spirits. We turn to passages like this just as we do with Psalm 23, Joshua 1:9, Romans 8:28, and a host of other passages that give us just the right dose of tonic when our souls feel most sickened.

On the other hand, we recognize just how hard this passage is to actually *apply*. Worry is not like a switch we can turn off, is it? Like its companion emotions, fear and grief, worry is one of those feelings that tends to grow the more we ignore it. When we try to make the conscious choice to not worry, we enter a kind of interpsychic tug-of-war, in which the energy required to ignore the source of our worry can actually make that worry grow even stronger. It's like pouring water on a grease fire. The more we try to douse it, the more intense it gets.

Jesus's command to not worry often comes at just the right time, in those moments when it is most difficult to apply it. His question is both comforting and complicating all at once.

Part of the tension comes from having free will. The freedom to choose is a gift from God. It enables us to act. We don't have to sit back and passively allow threats to overtake us. We can choose to respond—to fight or flee, to prepare or preempt, to react or respond. This is what we are wired to do, what God has equipped us to do.

The benefit of having free will is that we have the power to do something. But that is also its shadow side: we often feel the urgency to do something…even over things we can't control. That very free will can also be a precursor to worry.

After all, do you know what never has to worry about anything? Puppets. Puppets don't have to worry. They just move according to the hands that are controlling them. Same thing with robots. I've never met a worried robot.

When Jesus tells us to be like lilies and sparrows, like flowers and birds, we can admit that as lovely and serene a sentiment as that is, we enjoy being *unlike* lilies and sparrows. We like having free will. We need free will. We don't want to be exactly like lilies and sparrows.

We might read a passage like this one from Luke and wonder to ourselves, *What exactly is Jesus telling us about the relationship between worry and free will?* Does not worrying mean doing nothing? (Except avoiding a double negative, for sure.)

It would be good to remember that when God created humanity, we were given more than just the gift of free will. God gave us something just as valuable, and it is just as important to remember in times of anxiety. God gave us interdependence.

> *God made a universe in which each element and each creature interacts with the others to sustain the good of the whole.*

God created interdependence. God made a universe in which each element and each creature interacts with the others to sustain the good of the whole. The sun warms the planet, the moon triggers the tides, and the earth maintains the water cycle. The waters nourish the ground and give life to the seas. The world holds the balance of all of life, including human beings, who are entrusted to be stewards and caretakers of it all. Connecting all of life on this planet is the invisible but invaluable gift of air.

Lilies and sparrows cannot survive in isolation. Neither can any other living creature. Even human beings, with our vaunted free will and capacity to act by our own volition, cannot survive without a connection to the rest of the universe. The waters, sunlight, and organic material that nourishes flowers and birds are the very same factors that enable us to open our eyes every morning.

Interdependence is as important as free will, and it is just as much a generous gift from God. One way to look at Jesus's teaching is that we can face our anxieties by acknowledging with gratitude those aspects of our lives that are an undeserved gift.

Lilies and sparrows receive what they need through this gift of interdependence. Both need oxygen to convert to energy, water to hydrate them, and air to help them move and grow. Lilies and sparrows receive these things from God through the world God created. We, too, can acknowledge what we receive through interdependence. We, too, can be grateful for the simple gift of breath.

The word for *spirit* in both Hebrew (the original language of most of the Old Testament) and Greek (the original language of the New Testament) is related to the words for air, breath, and wind. The wind of God hovered over the face of the deep at creation. The breath of God filled the nostrils of the first humans, animating them from lifeless clay. The winds of God touched the earth at Pentecost and created a new living community of believers.

Through history, Christian mystics have believed that the simple act of breathing was itself a participation in the presence of God. It should be no surprise that when it comes to dealing with anxiety in the moment, one of the best things we can do is focus on our breathing.

After all, the word *anxious* comes from the Latin word *angere*, which means to choke or afflict. One way to understand anxiety is that it puts a kind of choke hold on you. It closes off your air supply, emotionally and mentally, and leaves you breathless. That same Latin word *angere* is also the root for words like *anger*, *angst*, and *anguish*. That figurative lack of air contributes to a whole spectrum of anxiety-related emotions, including grief, indignation, worry, sadness, isolation, you name it.

Often, the best way to address those anxious moments is through the simple, indispensable act of breathing.

Take a Breath

In his book *Breath: The New Science of a Lost Art*, science writer James Nestor chronicled his ten-year journey exploring the benefits and misconceptions of breathing. It began with his personal quest to learn how to overcome various health challenges he was facing, and it led him to interview various experts across different disciplines and cultures around the world. He suggests that "some of these researchers were also showing that many modern maladies—asthma, anxiety, attention deficit hyperactivity disorder, psoriasis, and more—

could either be reduced or reversed simply by changing the way we inhale and exhale."[1]

Nestor's book offers many practical insights and exercises into how to breathe better, along with compelling stories of people who experienced mental and physical improvement by breathing a different way. One of those persons is Alicia Meuret, a Southern Methodist University psychologist who teaches people to stifle the symptoms of asthmatic episodes and panic attacks with a simple but counterintuitive focus on their manner of breathing. Nestor writes, "To stop the attack before it struck, subjects breathed slower and less, increasing their carbon dioxide. This simple and free technique reversed dizziness, shortness of breath, and feelings of suffocation. It could effectively cure a panic attack before the attack came on. 'Take a deep breath' is not a helpful instruction,' Meuret wrote. 'Hold your breath is much better.'"[2]

Nestor concludes his book with a simple definition of "the perfect breath":

> Through all my travels and travails, there is one lesson, one equation, that I believe is at the root of so much health, happiness, and longevity. I'm a bit embarrassed to say it has taken me a decade to figure this out, and I realize how insignificant it might look on this page. But lest we forget, nature is simple but subtle.
>
> The perfect breath is this: Breathe in for about 5.5 seconds, then exhale for 5.5 seconds. That's 5.5 breaths a minute for a total of about 5.5 liters of air.[3]

It is no wonder that many ancient Christian mystics practiced "breath prayer" as a simple but effective spiritual discipline. In her book *Paths to Prayer: Finding Your Own Way to the Presence of God*, Patricia Brown shares one way to practice breath prayer based on Psalm 46:10. It is structured around an idea similar to Nestor's "perfect breath," inhaling and exhaling for counts of five. It also involves holding one's breath between each exhale and inhale, echoing Meuret's recommendation of allowing the buildup of carbon dioxide to relieve anxiety and stress. Brown also notes that Christian mystics believed that in those satisfying moments of taking in a full breath, the Spirit of God is most fully recognized. Holding that full, beautiful breath for a few seconds can be an act of resonance with God's presence.

A few years ago, Brown provided a workshop for our entire church leadership, and she led us in this guided exercise based on a chapter from her book:

> Take a moment now to put your feet flat on the floor. Don't cross your legs. Sit with your back straight and your palms on your lap, faceup or down. Close your eyes.
>
> Remember in this moment that God holds you in a loving presence, just as water fills every nook and cranny.
>
> Now, slowly count to five, taking in a deep breath: 1...2...3...4...5 and hold that breath in for a second or two. This is the place where the mystics say God dwells. Now begin to exhale slowly:

> 1...2...3...4...5 and hold for a second. Take
> another breath in, and another breath out.
>
> Continue that pattern of breathing, counting to five
> and holding it in silence; then listen to adaption of
> Psalm 46:10.

Brown then read each of the following lines, slowly, with enough time in between for people to take their five counts of inhaling, exhaling, and holding.

> Be still, and know that I am God... [pause]
> Be still, and know that I am... [pause]
> Be still and know... [pause]
> Be still... [pause]
> Be... [pause]
> [SILENCE]
> Now gently, slowly open your eyes. How are you
> feeling? As the Spirit releases you from this time of
> breath prayer, carry its calm awareness with you as
> you move on with your day.[4]

Breath prayers are an ancient spiritual practice whose effectiveness is corroborated by modern "pulmonauts" (James Nestor's term) studying the physiological benefits of proper breathing. Breathe in slowly and sparingly through the nose, breathe out slowly and fully through the mouth, and hold on to breaths in moments of tension.

Over the course of a lifetime, the average human being breathes 670 million times. That simple act is a reminder that, like lilies and sparrows, all living beings are connected to one another and to the Spirit, who gives us life.

Combating Anxiety with Gratitude

Another implicit aspect of Jesus's teaching on lilies and sparrows is gratitude. In reminding us that God gives birds and flowers all they need to survive, we ought to take regular moments to acknowledge and give thanks for all the little things God gives us that we take for granted.

In her book *Grateful: The Subversive Practice of Giving Thanks*, Diana Butler Bass explores the power of gratitude to shape both our emotions and our ethics, as individuals and as a community. She reminds us that *gratitude* and *grace* come from the same root word, *gratia* in Latin and *charis* in Greek. To be grateful in a spiritual sense is to acknowledge the unmerited favor of God, who gives us gifts of salvation, joy, provision, comfort, and hope without any expectation of return.

> *To be grateful in a spiritual sense is to acknowledge the unmerited favor of God, who gives us gifts of salvation, joy, provision, comfort, and hope without any expectation of return.*

That perspective makes gratitude less a transactional notion (you gave me a gift, so I am obligated to say thank you) and more an expression of wonder and delight. Gratitude can be a response to even the small and subtle blessings that we receive, and it can transform our reactions to suffering and hardship. Bass writes:

> All around us, every day, there are gifts. Whether we are facing a crisis or not, no matter our challenges or feelings, there are gifts, most of which go unnoticed, unappreciated, and often disregarded. Sometimes they take us by surprise—we experience the "aha" of being helped or suddenly seeing a beautiful sunset, and the emotion of gratitude wells up in our being. Gifts seem to spring upon us like an epiphany, bursting our hearts with that wild admixture of humility and joy that we know as gratitude.[5]

Among the practical exercises she gives is the practice of the daily examen, created by the Roman Catholic monastic order of the Jesuits. It is a way of looking back at the day honestly, acknowledging God's presence in the current moment, and looking ahead to the following day with clarity and hope. It includes five steps:

1. Become aware of God's presence
2. Review the day with gratitude.
3. Pay attention to your emotions.
4. Choose one feature of the day and pray from it.
5. Look toward tomorrow.[6]

John Wesley followed a similar practice on a weekly basis. In his book *Five Marks of a Methodist*, Steve Harper describes how Wesley would spend each Saturday evening conducting a "personal gratitude inventory."[7] He would consider three questions during that time.

1. Have I allotted some time for thanking God for the blessings of the past week?

That question is pretty straightforward. Have I been as thankful as I can be over these past several days? Did I focus solely on my problems, go about my busyness, and work myself to the bone to make it through the week, or did I remember to find time to be grateful to God for all that God has given me?

I suspect that for some Saturday nights, Wesley was able to say yes. But for most of us, if not all of us, we would have to admit that gratitude was neither a guiding principle nor a prevalent aspect of most weeks. Asking that question recalibrates our intention for the week ahead, and slowly, we can build up the spiritual musculature to make gratitude a more central aspect to our attitudes and behaviors.

As if that question alone weren't challenging enough, there are two more for us to ask ourselves about the past week's blessings.

2. Have I, in order to be the more sensible of them, seriously and deliberately considered the several circumstances that attended them?

This question is even tougher than the first. Wesley invites us to ponder, essentially, "Is it possible that God was blessing me even when I was at my lowest point this week? Is it possible that even when I was facing significant challenges, God was in fact still there to give me strength?"

Sometimes you can only see the hand of God at work when you are looking in the rearview mirror of life, when blessings are closer than they first appear. We often find that blessings are hard to recognize, but they are there nonetheless.

Wesley was not trying to minimize suffering and struggle or to trivialize their effects. Sometimes suffering just stinks, and there is no sugarcoating it. He wasn't trying to solve the problem of evil in the world, gain new understanding of why bad things happen to good people, or why the world is the way it is.

Instead, Wesley was just reminding himself every Saturday night that God was present in every moment among the "circumstances that attended them." An awareness of God's presence elicits the one thing that we can do when life makes us the most anxious. It is the one thing we can control because of God's strength. *We can choose to be grateful.*

Answers to both of these questions lead us to the ultimate outcome, captured in question three.

3. Have I considered each of them as an obligation to greater love, and consequently, to stricter holiness?

Another way to ask that question is, "In what way is God blessing me, even through the darkness and toughness of life, to be a blessing for someone else?" John Wesley believed that "there is no holiness apart from social holiness" and that the depth of our love for God ought to translate into a deep love for other people. Gratitude ought to serve as a hinge, a pivot point, that first acknowledges the blessings of God toward us, so that God can be a blessing to others through us.

This kind of weekly check-in of gratitude can center us on the task of serving and loving others, and it can lead us to channel gratitude outwardly. Gratitude can shape our emotions and our ethics as a private response to anxiety and a corporate determination to alleviate the anxiety of others.

Keeping Track of Gratitude

The Daily Examen and the weekly check-in by John Wesley have in common the keeping of a private gratitude inventory. For some, an effective way to maintain such an inventory is through a journal, whether hard copy or digital, that calls us to keep track of reasons to be grateful.

During a particularly hard season of my life, my therapist suggested that I slightly alter the way I was noting gratitude in my own private journal. I admitted to her that most of what I was writing down were common, general things that most people are thankful for. My family, my health, my career, and so on. She invited me to be more intentional and more specific about what I was thankful for. In a way, she was inviting me to consider Wesley's second question, to give deliberate consideration to the circumstances surrounding them.

She shared with me that experts who study the benefits of gratitude suggest that the more specific and detailed a person is when journaling, the greater the capacity becomes for noticing blessings moving forward. I decided to give it a try.

The next day, instead of writing in my journal the big-picture reasons I am grateful, I wrote the following:

> The feeling of freshly washed linens on my bed as I woke up in the morning.
>
> The synchronized way that the tails of both my dogs wagged when they saw me walk into the room.
>
> The ray of sunshine that peeked through the trees as I turned a corner during my morning walk,

just as I was listening to a beautiful song on my headphones.

Do you know what? My therapist was right. That one day alone has pushed me to notice more things that I can be thankful for every day. Like lilies who are clothed in splendor, and birds who are given enough to survive, we are inundated every day with clear, vivid, albeit sometimes small blessings that, cumulatively, can be more than enough to outweigh the anxiety we face each day.

Combating Anxiety with Action

Ultimately, our free will is a gift from God, and it can be useful in combating anxiety. We are not helpless in any situation. God has empowered us to be resistant, proactive, and prepared. Action can be a part of anxiety's antidote.

My favorite, most comical personal example of being prepared occurred several years ago. For many years my two daughters and I were big fans of *MythBusters*, a television show in which the hosts explored commonly held assumptions about everyday life. In one particular episode I watched with my daughter Grace, the two main scientists were testing various theories on what to do if you accidentally drive your car into a body of water.

With your car submerging and filling with water, what is the best thing to do to make sure you escape the car and survive?

Do you open the car door once you hit the water? It turns out, the answer is no. The water pressure holds the door shut. Do you try to roll down the window? Again, no. The same water pressure pushes the glass tightly against the frame, making it impossible to roll the window down. Do you wait until the car hits the bottom, then force the door open? No. While it's possible to escape, waiting so long is risky because there is not much air left.

As it turns out, the best thing to do is break the window using a specially designed car window hammer. Do you know what I'm talking about? It's a hammer that provides a lot of force in a precise point on the window, shattering the window's tempered glass and enabling you to swim out of the car quickly.

As soon as we saw that part of the episode, I turned to Grace and said, "We need one of those in the car!" And Grace, who is as big a worrier as I am, replied, "Yeah, we do!"

So, the next day, I went up the street to the local car parts store, bought a car window hammer, stuck it in the glove compartment, and felt totally prepared to beat the odds in the event of submerging the car in water.

I'd like you to know that at the time, we were living in Iowa.

Iowa. Thousands of miles from either ocean. In a town where there were no deep lakes and where the biggest body of water was a river that often was no more than a foot deep.

But just in case, I was ready with my hammer!

> **God has given us the power and initiative to rise up to meet potential challenges.**

We are not helpless. God has given us the power and initiative to rise up to meet potential challenges. Anxiety and worry can be helpful in that way, to push us toward preparation. But we should also remember the limits of that kind of control. Ultimately, we are not in control of everything. Much of what we worry about may not even happen. That's why Jesus told us not to worry about tomorrow, since tomorrow will have enough worries of its own.

I've heard it said that worrying is like sitting in a rocking chair. There is a lot of activity, but no real movement. A lot of incessant, repetitive energy, but no productivity. You can likely point to many times in your life when your mind has been engulfed in that kind of mental back-and-forth that has consumed you incessantly. Jesus offers us a different way. Remember the lilies and the sparrows. Be aware of the capacity and limits of your own power. Remember to breathe and to be grateful. Act on those things you can control, and surrender to God those things you cannot control.

Most of all, remember that God is with you.

Questions for Reflection

1. What do you think is the relationship between worry and free will?

2. How can a sense of interconnectedness and interdependence with all of life help your anxieties?

3. What breathing practices might help you worry less?

4. How will you pay more attention to things you can be grateful for?

5. What actions can you take to combat your worries?

CHAPTER
4

What
Do You
Live For?

CHAPTER

4

CHAPTER 4

What Do You Live For?

Mark 8:34-38

After calling the crowd together with his disciples, Jesus said to them, "All who want to come after me must say no to themselves, take up their cross, and follow me. All who want to save their lives will lose them. But all who lose their lives because of me and because of the good news will save them. **Why would people gain the whole world but lose their lives?** *What will people give in exchange for their lives? Whoever is ashamed of me and my words in this unfaithful and sinful generation, the Human One will be ashamed of that person when he comes in the Father's glory with the holy angels."*

(Mark 8:34-38, emphasis added)

The question Jesus posed in this chapter was asked rhetorically, but it requires our answer nonetheless: "Why would people gain the whole world but lose their lives?" It is not worth it to gain, achieve, or become anything that would result in the loss of true life, the life that God intends.

How we answer Jesus's question in real terms, in everyday life, is an important matter. It can shape our attitudes, perspectives, and most of all, our priorities. What are you really living for? What good will it do you if you spend your life pursuing things that ultimately do not matter, rather than discovering the true life God desires for you? These are questions we need to answer clearly, readily, faithfully, and regularly.

A quote attributed to Ralph Waldo Emerson captures this critical question in this way: "The gods we worship write their names on our faces; be sure of that. And a man will worship something...That which dominates will determine his life and character. Therefore, it behooves us to be careful what we worship, for what we are worshipping we are becoming." [1]

What are you worshipping, what are you becoming, and what are you really living for?

For Mark, the best and only answer is captured in one word: *cross*.

To explore Mark's point in its fuller context, let's look at the wider setting in his gospel. The end of Mark 8 is the exact halfway point of Mark's sixteen-chapter gospel, which means that all the action in the first half of Mark's gospel is leading up to this chapter's Scripture reading. If this were a play, this passage would be the act 1 finale, building suspense and offering foreshadowing for what is to come in the second act of the story of Jesus.

It is here that Mark, the great storyteller, leaves the disciples hanging with this ominous saying from Jesus: "All who want to come after me must say no to themselves, take up their cross, and follow me."

There it is. *Cross.* It's the central symbol of the Christian faith and a hallmark of Mark's gospel. Mark uses the word *cross* more than either Luke or John does, and the same number of times as Matthew despite being the shortest gospel. But this is the first time it's mentioned in the entire Gospel of Mark. Jesus waits until now, at the halfway point of his ministry, to mention anything about the cross for the first time.

Notice Jesus is not just referring to himself. He is not just saying, "We have to head toward Jerusalem now, because a cross is awaiting me there." That would be hard enough for the disciples to understand. Instead, he says something even more difficult: "There is a cross for you too. If you want to follow me, there is a cross for you to carry as well."

I guess we can understand why Jesus waited until now to mention it. Could you imagine how different the beginning of Mark's Gospel would have sounded, if back when Jesus was first calling the disciples, he had included the cross in that initial encounter?

For instance, imagine Mark 1:17, if Jesus had called the disciples and said, "Follow me, I'll show you how to fish for people, and you will experience persecution and hardship in the form of a cross."

"You guys with me? Anyone?"

I'm not so sure they would have said yes.

Imagine a local church redesigning its website to attract new visitors. Instead of a website that reads, "Excellent children's ministry," "Inspiring music," or "Seven steps toward a more joyful life," what if it read, "Join us and discover sacrifice, struggle, and hardship." How many clicks do you think that website would get?

Or imagine a church putting a banner on its front door that reads, "Join us and suffer!" How well would that go?

Frankly, it's a wonder that the disciples even decided to keep following Jesus at that point. We wouldn't blame them if they had deserted him halfway through his ministry. There was no mistaking what he was saying. If you want to follow Jesus, your cross is unavoidable. It is about losing what you value the most to gain what you do not understand.

It is here that he asks the central question of our chapter, one of the most poignant ones in the entire Gospel: *"Why would people gain the whole world but lose their lives?"*

Honestly, if it were you and me standing in the disciples' sandals that day, we would have seriously considered walking away right then and there. Imagine our response: "Wait a minute, Jesus. Are you saying this isn't about me? This isn't about meeting my needs? Are you saying this isn't about making me feel good? Or helping me feel powerful, happy, and successful? Wait—what?"

It's surprising anyone would bother to stick with him, given all the temptations in the culture to give us those very things: power, happiness, success. It raises this important question of you and me: "Why bother following Jesus at all?"

William Willimon, United Methodist bishop and former dean of Duke Divinity School's chapel, got a call one day from an angry parent. The man had sent his daughter off to college at Duke. She was supposed to be headed to graduate school but had just decided to throw it all away to, as he said, go do mission work with the Presbyterians in Haiti. He chewed out Dr. Willimon saying, "I hold you personally responsible for this."

"Me?" he asked. "That's absurd!"

The father shouted, "She has a BS degree in mechanical engineering from Duke University, and now she's going to dig ditches in Haiti?"

Willimon replied, "Well, I doubt that she received much training from the engineering department for digging ditches, but she is probably a fast learner and will get the hang of ditch digging in just a few months."

"Look," the parent said, "this is no laughing matter; you're completely irresponsible for encouraging her to do this."

Willimon said, "Now, wait just a minute! Aren't you the one who brought her to church and had her baptized?"

"Well, yes."

"And aren't you the one who brought her to church—to Sunday school, even, and to church on Sunday morning?"

"Well, yes."

"Aren't you the one who read Bible stories to her at night on occasion with your family? And let her go with that youth fellowship on the ski and mission trip in Vale?"

"Well, yes, but—"

"Don't 'but' me! It's your fault that she believed all that stuff and that she's gone and thrown it all away to Jesus, not mine. You're the one who introduced her to Jesus, not me."

The father then said, "But all we ever wanted her to be was a Presbyterian."

Willimon replied, "Sorry. You messed up and made her a disciple of Jesus Christ."[2]

That's how dangerous this question from Jesus is. How we answer it can change the trajectory of our lives. It can reorient our priorities and reframe how we see our way in the world. If we answer it correctly and choose to take up our cross and

71

forgo the ways of this world, then we can gain the only thing that matters.

Life. True life. A soulful life.

Gaining Your Soul

"Why would people gain the whole world but lose their lives?" The NRSVUE translates that verse as "For what will it profit them to gain the whole world and forfeit their life?" That word *life* is important. The Greek word behind it is *psyche*, from which we obviously get the words *psyche*, *psychology*, and *psychiatry*. It can mean "life" or "mind" but it can be also be translated as "soul."

We sometimes think of the soul as the part that continues existing after our bodies die, but that's not quite right. The Greek *psyche* means something deeper; it refers to the totality of our existence. The soul is deeper than just our brains and our minds, our ability to think thoughts and use reason. It is deeper than our hearts and our emotions, our ability to feel and emote and relate to others. It is deeper than our gut, our instinct, our drive, and our power.

Our souls are gifts from God.

The soul is the source of all that it means to be alive. It is what God gave us the very moment God breathed into us at our creation. Our souls are gifts from God.

Admittedly, that's still a bit of a fuzzy way to describe the soul. There is no quick and easy definition. Philosophers and theologians throughout history have attempted to describe it, see it, analyze it; yet the soul is still a mysterious part of our existence.

Despite the difficulty to describe it, you surely know you have a soul, especially when it is broken or fractured. Think about it: Have you ever had a moment when you felt your soul was crushed? You know what I mean: an episode in your life that was more than just head and heart stuff, more than just stressful in your mind, or saddening in your heart, or tiring in your body. I'm talking about those moments when you've felt all the energy just drained from your body, or an ache inside too deep for words, or a hurt so bad you can't describe it. That's your soul.

Maybe you've had the opposite kind of experience—soul-lifting, not soul-crushing. Perhaps you've had moments when you've felt so inspired, so overwhelmed, so grateful, that everything in your life—your body, mind, and heart—have all felt perfectly aligned and all was right with your world, even for just a moment. That is your soul that you are sensing.

If I were to offer you a two-part definition of the soul, the first part would be this: the source of our lives.

But there's another part to the definition. The soul is what draws us toward God. If the soul is a gift from God, given to us the moment we are created, then its function is to lead us into a closer relationship with God. It's like what happens when someone gives you a gift: the effect is that you feel a closer tie, a closer kinship to that person than you had before. Many times, the bigger the gift, the more significant the occasion, the greater the bond that is formed between the gift giver and the gift receiver.

Each of us has been given the most amazing gift of all: the gift of life itself. The gift of our identity, our passion, our personality, our emotions, our intellect, our abilities. Our soul. God has given all of that to you. The result of being given such a wonderful gift is that it draws us back to God, yearning to be in a relationship with God.

Consider Psalm 42:1: "As a deer longs for flowing streams, / so my soul longs for you, O God" (NRSVUE).

Consider the words of Saint Augustine in the opening paragraph of his *Confessions*: "You have made us and drawn us to yourself, and our heart is unquiet until it rests in you."[3]

And consider the words of the great hymn "How Great Thou Art": "Then sings my soul, my Savior God to thee; how great thou art, how great thou art!"[4]

So, here is a two-part definition of the soul. Our souls are the source of our lives that draw us into the Source of All Life.

Here's the concern: Our souls need to be nurtured. They need to be developed. Just like flowers in a garden, they need to be weeded, watered, and protected so they can blossom and grow to full beauty and full potential.

It is a particular challenge when we have faced traumatic moments in our lives that seem to crush our souls and burden our spirits. Still, our souls need to be tended, so that the Spirit can work fully and freely to draw us into a close, personal encounter with God.

I once heard this quotation: "The caterpillar is the most confused creature which roams the planet, because undoubtedly stamped in his soul is the call to fly."

Some of us can relate. We are confused and defeated, knowing that there should be more to our lives than what we have right now. We feel ashamed or guilty from our past. We feel hurt by the brokenness we feel inside. We feel unloved or unlovable. Some of us are just plain tired.

So, we strive. We push. We work hard day after day to seek some kind of happiness, a salve to soothe our anguished…souls.

But Jesus said those who seek their lives in this way will lose it. Those who lose their lives, those who surrender their souls to God, will discover true life.

So let us be as the deer, longing for flowing water, longing for God.

The Long View

Our soul's deep longing for God suggests one reason Jesus may have waited until this point to mention anything about the cross to the disciples. Jesus knew that spiritual maturity is not instantaneous. It is not a quick fix. It is a process that requires a lifetime of small steps, with each one capable of more stretching and growing than the one before. It is what Friedrich Nietzsche called "a long obedience in the same direction." He said, "The essential thing 'in heaven and in earth' is, apparently (to repeat it once more), that there should be long obedience in the same direction; there thereby results, and has always resulted in the long run, something which has made life worth living."[5]

What Jesus is saying to us today is that to gain the kind of life that God intends for us requires a series of losses. Not all at once, not all at the beginning of our lives or our spiritual journeys. Not in chapter 1 of our lives. That would make it too easy to walk away from God. Instead, God is there to guide us through one necessary hardship after another, all for the sake of our learning to trust in God more and more and to rely on our own agendas less and less. If it's true that with age comes wisdom, maybe it's also true that with hardship comes maturity.

I think we know this intuitively through basic life experience. We learn some of our most important lessons *later* in life, not as adolescents or teenagers. Sometimes it is not until further into adulthood, as we approach the halfway point, the Mark 8 of our own lives, when we can stretch without breaking and grow up without giving up.

We learn the value of loyalty by experiencing the sting of betrayal. We learn about long-term commitment after we go through heartbreak. We learn how to spot sincerity in others only by experiencing dishonesty and insincerity. We learn the power of grace when we learn from our biggest mistakes. We learn how to forgive when we are wounded more than we thought we could bear. We discover the limits of both flattery and criticism only when we learn the hard way not to believe our own press.

These are lessons that take time to learn. They are crosses that we learn to bear only when we are ready, and sometimes only when we learn the hard way.

We can't learn all these things when we are young, when we aren't strong enough, when we are unable to be stretched without breaking. These hard lessons come across a lifelong process, as a series of losses in moments when we can handle them. In that way, suffering can offer us a gift of increasing our capacity to hold pain, so that we can grow from it and help others to endure.

Yet Mark would remind us of one more very important truth. It is not just any suffering that can lead to true life. It is in losing one's life for Christ's sake that one can gain one's own life. As important as it is to learn all those other life lessons through hardship, it is even more important to mature in one's faith by taking up one's cross and learning to let go of everything else.

There's an old saying: Everybody wants to go to heaven, but nobody wants to die. Well, we may want the kind of life that God intends for us, but we may not want to let go of that which is necessary to attain it.

As urban legend has it, when Thomas Edison invented the light bulb, he got it right only after one thousand attempts. After he succeeded, he said that he hadn't failed 999 times; he had successfully found 999 ways that didn't work. Edison was convinced that the greatest barrier to his success was not the many times he failed, but his temptations to stop trying. He knew that the one thing that could prevent him from a breakthrough was sitting content with the way things were, instead of working, growing, and learning. What kept him going the first 999 attempts was the conviction that in every attempt was the possibility of a breakthrough.

God is not finished with you yet.

In much the same way, God is not finished with you yet. The process of taking up your cross is one that will take a lifetime of commitment, so that slowly but surely, you will see true life shine through you.

"The one who started a good work in you will stay with you to complete the job," Paul wrote to the church in Philippi (Philippians 1:6). When God looks at you, God sees light bulbs in your future. God sees moments in your spiritual journey when you will be able to live your life exactly as God intends it. There is a life for you that is filled with the love of

God, in which everything is finally in sync with God's best for you. It is a life filled with love for others, wherein your relationships are possible and serving others becomes as natural as breathing. It is a life of freedom from yourself as you become fully surrendered to God.

The only thing that can stand in the way of a light bulb moment in your spiritual life is your complacency, your contentment with how your spiritual life is now, or some belief that you just aren't capable of having God use you.

Going Deeper and Farther

Jesus told lots of stories about people like that. Once there was a person who owned a large piece of land. He took care of it, protected it, did everything right with it. Except for one thing: he didn't dig deeper. He was content with how things appeared on the surface, never realizing that hidden in plain sight the whole time, just under the surface, was a treasure hidden in the middle of his field. There was the possibility of a breakthrough if only he had dug deeper. Wherever you are in your spiritual journey, God isn't finished with you yet, and we are all called to take another step toward following Jesus, to go further in digging deeper in our commitment to Jesus, because God has a breakthrough in store for us. It's not too late.

One important way to gauge the growth of your commitment to Jesus is by evaluating your personal, private spiritual practices. We are most familiar with corporate disciplines, like worship, small group participation, and acts of service and compassion. At Hyde Park United Methodist, the church that I serve, we call those communal actions

"Worship, Small Groups, and Service," and we refer to them as the three corporate spiritual practices.

But there's more. Of the seven disciplines of our church's "discipleship pathway"—our prescribed method for growing in our faith—those first three are the easiest to publicly demonstrate our participation. A few years ago, we realized that it's the other four, the private practices, that are much more easily avoided and harder to keep accountable. No one knows how regularly we practice them except us and God.

So, to lift them up into our awareness, and to continue holding them out for the congregation to observe, we developed an acronym that helps us remember them: GRIP, which stands for Give, Read, Invite, and Pray.

1. Give financially in a way that is joyful and generous.
2. Read the Bible regularly without fear or frustration.
3. Invite others to Jesus in a way that is natural and unintimidating.
4. Pray with confidence and conviction. Believe that prayer really matters and makes a difference.

To grow deeper in your walk with Jesus, to refuse to let spiritual complacency block the light-bulb moments that God has in store for you, and to discover that treasure in you that has been hidden in your field all along, get a GRIP: Giving, Reading Scripture, Inviting Others, and Praying.

Give Generously

Jesus knew that for many people, financial generosity was the biggest barrier to living life as God intended it. He preached on it more often than almost any other subject. He knew something about us that we don't like to admit very often: As much as we may say we want God in our lives, in our public spheres, and in our country and world, the last place we want God is in our wallets. Jesus knew that for most of us, if we can learn to turn our financial life over to God, we can learn to give our whole life over to God.

This first private spiritual practice involves honoring God with your money. It is not just about honoring God with your thoughts and your actions. It is about honoring God with your finances. If you want to live life as God intends, it needs to start there.

As Paul said to the church in Corinth, "Everyone should give whatever they have decided in their heart. They shouldn't give with hesitation or because of pressure. God loves a cheerful giver" (2 Corinthians 9:7). Give of your finances with joy and generosity. God loves a cheerful giver.

Here is a practical piece of guidance for you to pray over, a goal for you to shoot for as you take the next step in giving. It's a simple principle called 10-10-80 that guides your relationship with money. Every time you receive a paycheck or any kind of income, think 10-10-80.

> 10: Ten percent goes to God. We call that a tithe.
> It is an act of worship and gratitude for
> what God has given you, and it is simply
> returning back to God what belongs to God
> to begin with.
>
> 10: Ten percent goes to savings. There are many
> stories in the Bible where people saved up in
> their storehouses for the future. Diligently

adding to your savings allows you to live in
freedom when the unexpected happens and
once you retire.

80: Eighty percent is for you to live on. Use this
money to pay your bills, to care for your
family and friends, and to spend with joy
on things you need and want.

None of this is rocket science. It is found in the Bible and
has been advocated by lots of Christian financial planners. It
is a framework for you to follow and work up to.

Read the Scriptures

If you want to cook a meal to perfection, follow the recipe.
If you're lost and want to find your way, check the map. If
you're wanting to assemble your newest purchase, follow
the instruction manual. And if you want to live life as God
intends it, read and apply the Bible to your life. It really is as
simple as that. And it really is as challenging as that.

For generations, people have found in the Bible
encouragement during trying times, comfort during grief,
and direction when they have been lost and wayward. It has
transformed the lives of people for thousands of years, and it
can do the same for you, just as it did for Augustine.

Before he became a saint, Augustine was a troubled,
rebellious person. As he recorded in his classic autobiography,
titled *Confessions*, one day he was outside his home, weeping
under a tree and crying in anguish:

> As this deep meditation dredged all my wretch-
> edness up from the secret profundity of my being

and heaped it all together before the eyes of my
heart, a huge storm blew up within me and brought
on a heavy rain of tears....Many things I had to
say to [God], and the gist of them, though not
the precise words, was: "O Lord, how long? How
long? Will you be angry for ever?...Why must I
go on saying, 'Tomorrow...tomorrow'? Why not
now? Why not put an end to my depravity this
very hour?"[6]

It is then that he heard a voice. It sounded like the voice
of a child, speaking in the distance, repeating the same phrase,
"Take up and read; take up and read." When he got up to
see where the voice was coming from, he found a book of the
apostle Paul's lying there. When he opened it up, Augustine
said, the pages turned to the Book of Romans. He read the
apostle's admonition to "put on the Lord Jesus Christ," and the
long struggle of his spiritual life was over. He opened himself
to God's love and forgiveness, and it changed his life forever.

The Bible is not just an anthology of stories. It is not just
a collection of pious phrases. This book contains the power to
transform your life, so that you can live it just as God intends.
All you have to do is "take up and read." Better yet, read it in
community with other people.

Granted, that is a lot easier said than done. We are busy
people, and parts of the Bible are confusing, even troubling.
But developing the spiritual musculature to read the Bible,
study it, and apply it will afford you this amazing benefit,
summarized in a single, five-letter word:

Story. You will discover your story.

Our brains often interpret the world in terms of stories,
and that includes the way you perceive your own life.

Whether you realize it or not, you see yourself as the star of your own story, and you want to live your story better. You are trying to be a good parent to your children. You are trying to overcome your obstacles to not only survive but thrive. You wonder what the next chapter, or even the next page, of your life will bring. You are trying to be the best hero of your story you can be.

> *Whether you realize it or not, you see yourself as the star of your own story, and you want to live your story better.*

We want to discover the best story that we believe God has called us to live, and there is no better way to live out that story than to discover it in the stories in the Bible. There are around seven hundred stories in this book, and each is an invitation for you to learn how to live out your own.

Are you fearful? There are stories there for you. Are you worried about your health? There are stories there for you. Do you want to be the best parent, or sibling, or family member you can be? There are stories there for you. Do you wonder where God is in the midst of your suffering? Find your story in the Bible. Are you confused about your future? Find your story in there. In fact, I remember when I was in college, I read and reread the story of Joseph in Genesis. It gave me encouragement to make it through a tough time in early adulthood. When I was struggling with matters of faith and doubt, I found myself in the story of Elijah on Mount Horeb. And when I needed to renew my passion for

Jesus, I discovered it in my early twenties when I reread the Resurrection story.

If you'd like a simple, structured way for you and others to read through the Bible together in a year, and to do so in a way that mitigates the fear and frustration that is commonly associated with reading the Bible, then I commend to you a book I wrote and accompanying program called *The Bible Year: A Journey through Scripture in 365 Days,* published by Abingdon Press. We created the curriculum for this program at our church and went on the journey in 2020. It continues to pay marvelous dividends for us as individuals and as a church.

Invite Others to Faith in Jesus

Inviting others to experience God's love revealed in Jesus is at the heart of what it means to be a follower of Christ. Just as Philip told Nathanael, "Come and see" after he met Jesus in John 1:46, we are called to invite others in a way that is natural and nonjudgmental, with a spirit of love and joy.

Penn Jillette is the verbal half of the world-famous magician duo Penn and Teller, and he is an outspoken atheist. He once told a story of a fan who came up to him after a show. They struck up a very friendly conversation, and then the fan began to talk to Penn about Jesus.

Penn described their encounter in this way: "It was really wonderful," he said. "I believe he knew that I was an atheist. But he was not defensive, and he looked me right in the eyes. And he was truly complimentary. It didn't seem like empty flattery. He was really kind and nice and sane and looked me in the eyes." In their conversation the person brought up the subject of Jesus and talked about his faith.

Penn's reaction was remarkable. Rather than disparage the guy for bringing up faith, he praised him. In the interview, he said that if you really believed that you have something that could benefit the life of someone else, that could help that person experience true life, you should share it. "How much do you have to hate somebody" not to reach out to them? Penn wondered. "I don't respect that at all. If you believe that there's a heaven and hell or whatever, and you think that it's not really worth telling them this because it would make it socially awkward, and atheists who think that people shouldn't proselytize—'Just leave me alone, keep your religion to yourself.' How much do you have to hate somebody to not [invite them]?"[7]

I find his words to be a gentle yet challenging reminder for Christians. If an outspoken atheist believes that Christians should care enough about others to invite them to Jesus, then we have little excuse for not doing just that.

Guy Kawasaki is the former marketing guru who worked at the Apple corporation in the 1980s. I love his title when he worked there. He was one of Apple's "software evangelists." It was his job to get people to fall in love with Apple. Not just to fall in love with their products, but to fall in love with a kind of life Apple's products could help them live. He wanted people to see Apple not just as another computer company, but as the key to living a life of comfort, convenience, and coolness by being part of the Apple community.

Kawasaki said this wasn't planned, but the effect was dramatic. They had so many "accidental customer evangelists" that they developed thousands of self-organized user groups. "Those are truly the evangelists," Kawasaki said. "They're not paid. They're not employees. They tell people to use

Macintosh solely for the other person's benefit. That is the difference between evangelism and sales. Sales is rooted in what's good for me. Evangelism is rooted in what's good for you."[8]

I love that. Not to disparage anyone who does sales for a living, but I love the way both an atheist magician and a corporate marketer know more about why Christians should be invitational than many of us Christians.

If we really believe that in Christ we can live life fully the way God intends it, a life full of love for God and others, then why shouldn't we share that?

Pray Regularly

Prayer is the lifeblood of our spiritual commitment. It guides our minds and centers our hearts in Jesus in a way that strengthens us to do all the other spiritual practices. But it can also be the most mysterious and the most challenging of the spiritual disciplines.

I think part of the difficulty that we sometimes have with prayer is that the way we first learned to pray, perhaps as children, feels like an odd way to pray as adults. As children, we were limited in our abilities to picture God, so we thought about God as an elderly-looking man up in the heavens, to whom we could talk using the right kinds of words. But now that we're adults, we wonder about the efficacy of those kinds of prayers.

We begin to wonder if prayer is just a psychological exercise in sorting through our thoughts. Or if prayer is little more than glorified meditation, in which we let our minds take a nap in the midst of busyness. Or if prayer is simply talking to ourselves and thinking things over. Because the moment we drift away from this idea that God is some old man in a robe up in heaven, we might wonder what prayer really means at all.

So how about an alternative view of God that might make prayer more meaningful?

One of the most formative books I've ever read on the subject of prayer is called *In God's Presence: Theological Reflections on Prayer*, by a contemporary theologian and author named Marjorie Suchocki.

In that book, Suchocki says,

> "Think of water as a different metaphor for God. Water rushes to fill all the nooks and crannies available to it; water swirls around every stone, sweeps into every crevice, touches all things in its path—and changes all things in its path. The changes are subtle, often slow, and happen through a continuous interaction with the water that affects both the water and that which the water touches."[9]

If that's a helpful image for God, then that means God is not above us or separated from us, but among us, around us, and within us. That makes prayer less about talking to someone on high and more about sensing God's presence and interacting with it as close as our own breath. As I said in an earlier chapter, the Hebrew word for *breath* also can mean "spirit." You are a spiritual being as much as you are a physical one, and the longing to connect to God is part of what it means to be alive.

Prayer is also more than simply connecting to God around you. It is also about connecting in community to other people.

Notice that the Lord's Prayer does not begin with "My Father," but "Our Father" (Matthew 6:9). It is a reminder that prayer connects us with one another, mutually sharing our identity in God. Not one of us is more or less important than another. All of us share in being children of God.

If you want your prayer life to connect you in love and relationship with other people and with God, then consider something called the five-finger prayer. It is a simple prayer that you can do with your children or with your eyes open.

Take either hand and look at it. First look at your thumb. It's the strongest and most important finger, and it's a reminder for you to pray for those who are closest to you, the ones easiest for you to remember. Pray for those people now.

Second, look at your index finger. They are the ones who point you in the right direction. They are the ones you count on for guidance: the teachers, guides, and models who exemplify for you the way to live. Pray for those people now.

Third, look at your middle finger. It is the tallest finger, so it reminds us to pray for those who are our civic leaders, the ones who are in authority over us. Pray for those people now.

Fourth, look at your ring finger. It is our weakest finger, and it is a reminder for us to pray for those who are weakest and most vulnerable and the ones who are suffering from hardship, injustice, and violence. Pray for those people now.

Finally, the smallest finger, the pinky, is a reminder to pray for yourself last. Pray for your own needs, those things that are affecting you right now.

Prayer need not be stale, rote, or sterile. It is a conduit through which you can be in touch with the presence of God in you and around you, like water flowing all around you. And it is my hope that you will learn to make the practice of prayer a regular part of your life. That is a priority for every follower of Jesus.

> *God is calling you to take up your cross, follow Jesus, and discover the truest, fullest life that God intends for you.*

God is not finished with you. God is calling you to take up your cross, follow Jesus, and discover the truest, fullest life that God intends for you. It means taking your personal spiritual practices seriously. Get a GRIP: Give generously, read the Bible, invite others to Jesus, and pray. And even if you have taken 999 steps before this one, keep going. Take that next step. Because God has a light-bulb moment, ready for you.

Questions for Reflection

1. What things are you pursuing in your life that are keeping you from taking up your cross and gaining life as God intends?

2. When has your soul felt crushed, and when has it felt lifted?

3. What important life lessons did you learn only later in life when you were ready? What lessons could you have only learned the hard way?

4. What private spiritual practices (GRIP) will you work on more diligently?

CHAPTER
5

Whom Will You Love?

CHAPTER 5

Whom Will You Love?

Luke 6:27-36

"But I say to you who are willing to hear: Love your enemies. Do good to those who hate you. Bless those who curse you. Pray for those who mistreat you. If someone slaps you on the cheek, offer the other one as well. If someone takes your coat, don't withhold your shirt either. Give to everyone who asks and don't demand your things back from those who take them. Treat people in the same way that you want them to treat you.

"If you love those who love you, why should you be commended? Even sinners love those who love them. If you do good to those who do good to you, why should you be commended? Even sinners do that. If you lend to those from whom you expect repayment, why should you be commended? Even sinners lend to sinners expecting to be paid back in full. Instead, love your enemies, do good, and lend expecting nothing in return. If you do, you will have a great reward. You will be acting the way children of the Most High act, for he is

> *kind to ungrateful and wicked people. Be compassionate just*
> *as your Father is compassionate."*
>
> (Luke 6:27-36)

Typically, when I meet with families to plan the funeral of a loved one, I eventually get around to asking whether that person had a favorite Bible verse, a meaningful text of Scripture that he or she turned to for comfort, wisdom, or guidance throughout life. I ask, of course, because I want to be sure to have it read during the service. But I also ask because it's the kind of question that reveals a great deal about a person's faith, character, and perspective on life.

It is interesting to me that many times over the years, families have said that their loved one chose this chapter's Scripture passage as one of their favorites. It is popularly coined the "Golden Rule," and I am sure you know it by heart and have uttered it often. Simply put, it says, "Do unto others as you would have them do unto you."

It is the closest thing to a bumper sticker sound bite that Jesus ever gave. It is short, quaint, pithy, and a tidy reminder of how we are to treat other people. To many people in congregations I have served, the Golden Rule evokes nostalgia for a bygone era, in which people's words were their bond, they could be trusted, and dignity and decency were the order of the day. I think this is why the families of so many people I have eulogized have named this passage as their favorite.

We often associate this passage with respecting others. Treat others fairly, just as you want others to treat you fairly. Honor your word and keep your promises because you wouldn't want to be lied to. Be trustworthy, kind, compassionate—all the kinds of things you'd hope others would do for you.

Throughout the centuries, the Golden Rule has been expressed in different ways, even by different religions. Confucius said, "Do not do to others what you do not want them to do to you." The Taoist thinker Lao-Tse said, "To those who are good (to me), I am good; and to those who are not good (to me), I am also good; ... and thus (all) get to be good."[1] In Islam, Muhammad said, "None of you has faith until he loves for his brother or his neighbor what he loves for himself."[2]

Every major religion has some version of the Golden Rule as one of its major tenets. It should be no surprise that when Jesus was offering his greatest teaching, known as the Sermon on the Mount, he included it in its simplest and cleanest form the way we commonly hear it and refer to it today.

We call it the Golden Rule, even though the Bible doesn't use that term, and we aren't certain as to the origins of its usage. One popular theory is that in the third century, the Roman emperor Alexander Severus liked the phrase so much he adopted it as his motto, displayed it on public buildings, and even wrote it in gold on his palace wall.

Regardless of why we call it the Golden Rule, the name has certainly taken hold in the cultural vocabulary of our time. It has become so deeply ingrained into the ethical subsoil of our culture that even the secular world knows it and refers to it.

A few years ago, the major hotel chain Marriott rolled out a national campaign promoting its customer service and espousing its high level of hospitality. Its thirty-second ad was called "Golden Rule" and featured images of Marriott employees treating guests with warmth and welcome. It begins by imagining how great it would be if humans were good at being human. The narration continues with aspirational ideas about neighbors being neighborly, people sharing generously, and an end to greed and selfishness. It then ends with these words:

> It would be spectacular if the golden rule was
> golden to every man
> And the good things that we ever did was
> everything we can.[3]

What I like about that ad is that it reminds us that even though the Golden Rule is simple, it is not easy. Even though every major religion espouses it, and even though our secular world—and even our corporate marketing world—promotes it, why do we still live in a world with such pain? Why is there such brokenness among us, among countries, and among religions? Why are there still so many heartbreaking news headlines about the violence and atrocities we commit against each other? Why do you and I have such brokenness in our relationships with loved ones, friends, coworkers, and even fellow Christians in the church?

It's because even though the Golden Rule is simple to understand, it is not easy to apply.

It's also because it is far too easy to forget what the Golden Rule really requires of us.

One of the ways it is commonly misunderstood and misapplied is to think of it as reciprocal, as transactional. If I scratch your back, I expect you to scratch mine, and I hold it against you if you don't.

In fact, Jesus addresses that misconception directly in the central question of this chapter: "If you do good to those who do good to you, why should you be commended? For even sinners do that." The Golden Rule is difficult to practice because it calls us to seek the betterment of others regardless of whether they do the same for us in return. Jesus said, "Love your enemies, do good, and lend expecting nothing in return."

The other way we commonly misunderstand the Golden Rule is by viewing it entirely egotistically. If I only treat you the way I want to be treated, then my primary filter for evaluating what is best for you is based on what I think is best for me. Here's a simplistic example. If you love fresh coffee and your spouse hates coffee but loves orange juice, the Golden Rule does not mean you serve your spouse coffee because you like it, even though he or she hates it. It means giving your spouse orange juice because you know that if you were your spouse, you would want orange juice.

In other words, the Golden Rule is misunderstood when we use our own personal desires and wishes as the primary filter to decide what is good and best for other people. That's why the Golden Rule has been supplemented by something called the Platinum Rule: "Do unto others as they would want you to do to them."

Those are wise words too. We immediately recognize that one ingredient is critical to helping us understand the best way to apply the Golden Rule. It is also the piece that is lacking in so many of our interactions with other people. If we practiced this one thing more regularly in our interactions with others, especially those who are different from us, it would make the practice of the Golden Rule so much more effective and beneficial. It might even change the world.

What is that ingredient? Empathy.

Empathy is our capacity to see the world and the situation through the eyes and perspective of another person. It means the removal of our own personal filters in order to put on the filter of the other person. To do that is often difficult, risky, and requires our vulnerability. To be empathetic, you first have to view that other person as a fellow child of God, someone with wounds and vulnerabilities, just like you, a person formed by his or her childhood and experience just as you have been. A person who has much more in common with you than you think.

It also means listening to the other person. It means standing by his or her side to approach a common goal in solidarity, not in opposition.

Advertising Empathy

Another fascinating commercial is called "Worlds Apart" by the Heineken Corporation. The fact that it is a beer commercial is only incidental to the larger, more provocative meaning and deeper message of the commercial. The premise is that three pairs of individuals, total strangers to each other, are put in a room with the task of building an object together. They know nothing about the task until they look at the plans. They also know nothing about each other at first. But we do. Before they meet, they share with the camera—and us—who they are and what they believe.

One pair involves two people with dialectically opposed views on climate change. A second pair includes two individuals with very different perspectives on feminism. A third pair includes both a transgender person and a man with strong views against transgender people.

In each case, none of these qualities are known by the other person when they first meet each other in the commercial. Instead, they begin the task of building their large mystery object together. During the first break period, they are asked to describe themselves to their partners in five words. Some of them choose words such as "opinionated," "frustrating," "dedicated," or "lucky," again without revealing any of their ideological or political perspectives.

They are then asked to discover three things they have in common as partners. In these remarkable exchanges, they discover mutual interests, passions, and personality traits, all while not knowing how ideologically different they are. They discover instead each other's humanity, and we get the sense that true friendships may be starting to bloom.

In the final scene of the four-minute, twenty-five-second commercial, we discover, much to the pairs' surprise, that they have constructed a bar. Stools and a cooler filled with beers stand at the ready.

It is then that the real clincher occurs.

Each pair then watches two short films, recorded in advance, of each individual revealing his or her own strong, conflicting opinions about hot-button issues. They then hear a voice:

"You now have a choice. You may go or you can stay and discuss your differences over a beer."

By the end of the commercial, and by the end of this journey of discovery of each other's humanity, each pair decides to stay, continue the conversation, and enjoy each other's company.[4]

Maya Angelou said, "We all have empathy. We may not have enough courage to display it."[5] It is that piece, our willingness to display empathy, that determines whether we practice the Golden Rule in the way Jesus intended it, or whether we warp the Golden Rule into something that is much more self-seeking and ultimately harmful.

It is not easy, which is why we must always seek the guidance, grace, and power of God. For it is only by God that we can do unto others what we would want them to do to us, and do for them what they would want of us.

Loving Our Enemies

To go one step further, we should acknowledge that this teaching of Jesus demands even more of us than just doing nice things for one another. It is about more than kindness, respect, and decency, as hard as those things may be on their own. Once we dig a little deeper, we discover that the context of these words makes them a lot more troubling, a lot more challenging, and a lot more complicated than they first appear.

Read again the entire passage from Luke. Notice that "the Golden Rule" is stated at the tail end of some truly riveting words from Jesus about people who are hard to love. He is not just talking about being nice to people and respecting others. He is talking about dealing with those in your life who have hurt you, caused you harm, and inflicted pain in your life. It is to those of you who have trouble forgiving that Jesus gives his prescription to do unto others as you would have them do unto you.

Make no mistake: the Golden Rule is about practicing forgiveness of those people who have hurt you so bad that you just want to lash back in vengeance.

It's here that Jesus gets downright cryptic, with some cultural references that seem odd and perplexing to us.

If someone strikes you, turn the other cheek.

If someone takes your cloak, give that person your shirt.

If someone forces you to walk a mile, go a second mile.

These are passages we'd prefer to just ignore, not because they are hard to understand but because they are unmistakably difficult to apply. Why would we want to turn the other cheek, give the shirts off our backs, and walk a mile further? Wouldn't that be a show of helplessness, weakness, and just plain giving up? What do we do with these passages?

Walter Wink, the great teacher and writer on the topics of nonviolence and spiritual warfare, wrote a terrific piece about how to understand the original cultural context of these verses.[6] Allow me to summarize what Wink has to teach us.

Turn the Other Cheek

Jesus said, "If someone slaps you on the cheek, offer the other one as well." It is significant that Jesus specified the right cheek, rather than the left.

To strike another person, one could use either a closed fist or an open hand. Fists were used in fights between combatants considered equal adversaries. Backhands, done with an open palm, were used to demonstrate power differentials and as a gesture of humiliation and dehumanization. Masters backhanded slaves; men backhanded women; parents backhanded children. One would never backhand a person he or she perceived as an equal. To humiliate someone, put the person in his or her place, and reprimand an inferior, use a backhand. In fact, in Jesus's culture, there was a stiff penalty for backhanding an equal, but none for backhanding an inferior.

Add to this the notion that back then, the right hand was the dominant hand, and the left hand was reserved for unsavory tasks, like conducting hygiene after relieving oneself.

The left hand was never used in eating. In fact, even to gesture with the left hand was punished with ten days' penance at the community of Qumran.

So, when backhanding someone, the right hand, not the left, was always used. And the only way to hit a person with the back of your right hand was to strike his or her right cheek.

Put all these pieces together and remember that what we are seeing in this passage is not a fistfight, but a derogatory insult by a person in power.

So, here is what Jesus was teaching his followers to do when they are backhanded by a so-called superior. Rather than hit back, rather than resort to violence (which would be a sure path to punishment by death), Jesus offered a clever and notable answer.

Turn your head and offer your left cheek to your attacker.

How would that person strike your left cheek? It would be physically difficult, if not impossible, for the attacker to backhand your left cheek with his or her right hand. Remember: using a left hand for such a purpose would have been inappropriate. So, the only option would be to use the fist of his or her right hand.

That action would essentially be a declaration that the two of you are equals. Fistfights are for equals; backhands are for inferiors. By turning the cheek, the victim is saying to the perpetrator, "I deny you the power to humiliate me. I am a human being. You cannot take away my self-respect." What it means to turn the other cheek is to maintain your dignity, to preserve your self-respect. Jesus was telling his followers, and telling us, that rather than resort to violence, the victim should remove the initiative from the perpetrator by declaring his or her dignity and worth for all to see, leaving the other person with no recourse.

Give Away Your Shirt

The second example of how to turn the tables and take the initiative in a nonviolent way is this: "If someone takes your coat, don't withhold your shirt either." Typically, we understand this passage to mean a gesture of generosity. When someone asks you for something, you are to give more than asked. Again, when we consider the culture of the ancient Near East, we discover that this is not what Jesus was teaching. He was pointing us toward a remarkably effective, nonviolent response to oppression.

The people of Jesus's day lived in a time of profound economic, judicial, and societal inequality. The great and powerful Roman Empire taxed people heavily to finance its army, wars, and expansions. This resulted in an economic system in which poor people had to borrow money at exorbitant interest rates to pay their taxes, feed their families, and survive. In the process, they often lost their land, their possessions, and even the very clothes on their backs. At times, people would be so indebted that they had to put up their own clothes as collateral. Jesus was referring to instances when people would have to give up their coats, their outer clothing, in desperation.

The other factor to consider is that in Jesus's time, public nudity was taboo. So, Jesus was teaching his followers that when the system has brought you to the lowest point of humiliation and dehumanization, and the oppression has removed your coat…give up your shirt.

In other words, your forced nakedness would expose the injustice of the system to the wider public. It would be an act of defiance ("You want my coat? Here: take my shirt. Now all I have left is my body. Do you want that too?"). It would also draw the public's attention, evoking not just laughter at you, but even more laughter at the person in power who put you in that position. Laughing at tyrants disarms them. Ridiculing the system can be the first step toward change.

Just as with the first teaching, on turning the other cheek, Jesus here was telling his disciples to turn the tables, without resorting to violence, to affirm their dignity and direct public scrutiny against the oppressor.

Though he advocated for nonviolence, Jesus did not endorse the idea that victims should just curl up into a ball and give in to bullies. Forgiveness does not mean letting the perpetrator walk all over you or being in denial about the pain it has caused you.

Instead, Jesus calls you to be courageous, creative, and diligent in responding to the harm someone has caused you. Respond to the evil that has been done to you with a disarming, surprising amount of compassion, and don't respond to violence with violence.

Forgiveness does not mean going back to the way things were before. It involves naming the hurt, not shying away from it, and addressing the perpetrator so as to acknowledge what has been done to you, but in the end, inviting repentance, healing, and reconciliation.

Walk the Extra Mile

A well-known third part of this trilogy of teachings is Jesus's directive to "walk the extra mile," even though it does not appear here in Luke's gospel. It is recorded in Matthew 5:41: "When they force you go to one mile, go with them two."

Again, this does not mean acquiescing to the oppressor in a helpless display of weakness. Jesus was advocating for a shrewd, nonviolent way of pointing out the injustices of the system for all to see.

This teaching centers on how, in the first-century Roman world, centurions would sometimes force oppressed people to carry their equipment for them. Innocent civilians would then have to drop their own possessions on the ground, leaving those items vulnerable to damage or theft. Such actions by heartless military were clearly abuses of the power differential that existed between a militarized state and a subjugated people, including the Jews of Galilee and Judea.

At the same time, there was also a cultural expectation in those days that centurions were not to allow someone to carry their equipment beyond one mile. It would have been publicly perceived as inhumane to expect people to carry the burdens beyond that, and it would have brought public scorn on those centurions.

In instructing followers of Jesus to "go the extra mile" would have meant willingly carrying the burden of the oppressor into public view, even just a few steps beyond what was culturally appropriate, to expose their injustices and highlight the inequities. Rather than advocating for violence to overcome violence, he showed his followers how to overcome injustice by bringing it to the light. Such teachings were formative to some of our greatest advocates for peace with justice through nonviolence, including Gandhi, Martin Luther King Jr., and Nelson Mandela.

It is certainly not easy to love our enemies. It is hard to practice the Golden Rule. And Jesus's question, "If you love those who love you, what credit is that to you?" is one we may wish he had never posed. But getting the answer right can be a key to transforming our lives, our relationships with others, and even the world's injustices.

The Power of Forgiveness

In 2012, an eighteen-year-old named Takunda Mavima appeared in court to hear a judge sentence him for the accidental deaths of seventeen-year-old Tim See and fifteen-year-old Krysta Howell, passengers in the car that an intoxicated Mavima crashed while driving home from a party in Wyoming, Michigan.

Having pled guilty to all charges, Mavima stood tearfully before the judge and repented: "I'm so sorry that I took two bright, intelligent, wonderful people out of this world....I wish . . . I'm so sorry."

One of the victim's sisters then stood before the judge and spoke these astonishing words of forgiveness and mercy: "I am begging you to let Takunda make something of himself in the real world—don't send him to prison and get hard and bitter, that boy has learned his lesson a thousand times over and he'll never make the same mistake again." And as Mavima was walking out of the courtroom, the victim's father stood up, went over to Mavima, and gave him a hug.[7]

Mavima was given a prison sentence of thirty months to fifteen years for his crime but was released after two and a half months. Upon his release, he was interviewed by a local program about that moment when the victims' families reached out in love and forgiveness to him in the aftermath of the accident.

"There's never a moment when I'm not thinking about that moment, because the love that the families have shown since the beginning has been so . . . immaculate. It's been so divine. It's God-given. These people opened their arms to me, no questions asked. It was unbearable. I couldn't believe it, that they weren't coming after me, because that's the way I felt about myself. I was putting myself down so much that I couldn't believe that these people of all people were showing me this amount of love. So, forgiveness changed my life."[8]

Mavima entered college and has become a motivational speaker to talk to youth about making responsible choices and claiming their best future.

Several years ago, in a Sikh temple in Wisconsin, a lone gunman motivated by white supremacy took the lives of six people and injured four others. Two days later, there was a candlelight vigil where residents in the community joined with Sikh faithful to remember the victims.

Observers were amazed by the response of the Sikh congregation. Instead of anger, revenge, or bitterness, Sikh congregants were unified in their message of forgiveness for the shooter.

Police chief John Edwards was among those amazed by their response. He recalled that in twenty-eight years working in law enforcement, he's seen a lot of anger, revenge, and hatred. The Sikh community, he said, did not demonstrate any of those things in the wake of the shooting. Instead, he saw an unusual response of compassion, concern, and support.

Teri Pelzek was one of the Oak Creek residents who was startled by the Sikhs' reaction. "It surprised everyone when they were victims of someone so full of hatred. Because of their reaction, saying they'd like to forgive and move on, I think that's quite the attitude to hear after what just happened....I knew nothing about them at all. I don't think a lot of people did. When we don't know about somebody's religion we assume the worst."[9]

Make no mistake: when Jesus said to do to others as you would have them do to you, he was talking about the long, hard, and risky road of forgiveness. No, it won't always be easy, but in the end, it is always worth it. For after all, isn't forgiveness what Jesus did for you and me? Since we are made in the image of that same Christ, can't we try a little harder to love those whom we have a hard time loving? Can't we learn to forgive?

Questions for Reflection

1. Who do you know who has modeled the Golden Rule for you?

2. How do you prevent the Golden Rule from being applied egotistically or reciprocally? In other words, how can you treat a person the way he or she wants to be treated rather than the way you want to be treated?

3. What are some ways you can strengthen your capacity for empathy for other people?

4. How will you learn to love those who are hard for you to love and forgive those who have harmed you?

5. Which of these three teachings of Jesus—turn the other cheek, give away your shirt, walk a second mile—is easiest for you to understand and apply? Which is hardest?

CHAPTER
6

What Are You Looking For?

CHAPTER

6

CHAPTER 6

What Are You Looking For?

John 1:35-38

The next day John was standing again with two of his disciples. When he saw Jesus walking along he said, "Look! The Lamb of God!" The two disciples heard what he said, and they followed Jesus.

When Jesus turned and saw them following, he asked, **"What are you looking for?"**

They said, "Rabbi (which is translated Teacher), where are you staying?"

(John 1:35-38, emphasis added)

The final question in our journey is the first one Jesus asked in the Book of John. It would be the first question of many in this Gospel, as no other writer relies on questions to the extent John does to tell the story of Jesus. Jesus asked two men, "What are you looking for?"

113

In the broadest sense, this last question is one of the most prominent and most important in the human experience. It is a question about desire and longing, not for temporal possessions or pleasures, but for ultimate meaning and purpose. It gets to the question we begin asking as children when we wonder what we will become when we grow up. It tugs at us when we venture into adolescence and discover our identity and personhood. We push into adulthood with this question at our heels, pondering our careers and life choices. At the end of our lives, it is one of the greatest remaining questions we answer as we look in the rearview mirror.

What did my life amount to? Did I find what I was looking for?

It is no wonder that this is the first question Jesus asked in the Gospel of John. It is that important to John's story, just as it is important to our lives. It is a fitting conclusion to our survey of Jesus's questions, and one that requires an answer as our journey draws to a close.

Jesus asked this question of two men, the first of whom was named Andrew (see verse 40). We don't know the other person's name; some scholars suggest he was John the gospel writer himself. What we do know about these two is that they were originally followers of a prophet named John the Baptist. John was an unorthodox preacher, to say the least. His teaching circuit was in the wilderness, his liturgical clothing made of camel's hair, and his diet consisting of locusts and wild honey. Nonetheless, he was a prophet with a following, including Andrew and his friend.

These men followed John as disciples often followed a rabbi or teacher. In ancient Judaism, being the disciple of a rabbi was no small thing. It was a long and involved process.

To be a follower of a rabbi meant much more than reading his books or being a fan or following him on social media. It took years to become a disciple of a rabbi. For many, it began as early as age five, when children first learned the Scriptures and became conversant in the faith. By age thirteen, at the time of the bar mitzvah, boys were expected to have the Torah memorized and be ready to begin the next phase of training. The teenage years involved additional intense instruction, called "the yoke of Torah." And by age seventeen, only those showing particular promise could be *selected* by a rabbi to become his followers.

If you were privileged enough to be selected by a rabbi to be a disciple, your journey would just be beginning as you started an apprenticeship that would take you years into your adulthood.

It has been said that a new disciple would hear these words as he ventured off into his new apprenticeship: "May you be covered by the dust of your rabbi." It was a word of blessing, admonition, and encouragement for the new disciple to follow his rabbi so closely, sit at his feet when he was teaching, model his behavior so accurately, and listen to his words so intently that he would be covered by the teacher's very dust.

That's what it meant to be a disciple of a rabbi.

So, in John 1:35, when we hear that Andrew and his friend were disciples of John the Baptist, we know that they had already invested much of their lives in following John. Up until then, to return to an image we used in chapter 1, their two circles were in perfect sync and harmony. The circle of their life experiences was a perfect match for the circle of their view of God. (We'll review this image of the circles shortly.)

115

Then one day, something happened to them. Jesus showed up. Their world was about to change, and their soon-to-be-former teacher, John the Baptist, knew it. John pointed to Jesus and basically said, "Fellas, it's time for your theology to grow. It's time for your idea of God and your view of the faith to mature. It won't be easy, because change of any kind is hard. But this man is the one to lead you there."

When Andrew and his friend turned to Jesus, that's when Jesus asked them a question, as any good rabbi would do:

"What are you looking for?"

The Two Circles Revisited

In chapter 1, we explored the image of two circles, and we would do well now to bring that image back full circle (pun intended) and revisit it one more time.

The first circle represents our life experience: the way we see the world and how we see our place in it. The other circle represents our view of God. It encompasses what we know and believe about the faith. Imagine again superimposing those circles on top of each other, aligning them with each other.

There may have been moments in your life when both circles have been a perfect fit. When your image of God and your understanding of the faith have matched perfectly with the events of your life and the conclusions you make of them. Those are moments of ease, security, and contentment. But those moments are often temporary.

You and I know that the circle of our life experience is never permanent. Life happens. We go through crises. We undergo hardship. We hear new, provocative ideas that challenge some of our assumptions. We see how our old ways of thinking cause harm.

As that circle of life experience expands, it causes tension with the circle of our theology. We discover that our view of God is not expansive enough. Those points of friction between the reality of life and the claims of our faith become troublesome and even painful.

That's when our spiritual life and our theology need to expand, grow, and mature.

The question Jesus asked Andrew and the other disciple came at a critical moment of their lives. It was at the crossroads of their journeys, when much of what they had learned under John the Baptist needed to adapt and shift in order to encompass a wider view of God's kingdom under Jesus.

So, when Jesus asked them, "What are you looking for?" he was really asking them, "Which of your former assumptions need to be challenged, to make room for the new thing that God wants to reveal to you?" In other words, this last question of Jesus was designed to get these two men to admit what questions they were pondering themselves, deep inside.

> *We cannot grow the circle*
> *of our theology on our own.*
> *We need God to guide us and*
> *nudge us to expand that circle.*

It is in this moment in our lives when God steps in, because we cannot grow the circle of our theology on our own. We need God to guide us and nudge us to expand that

117

circle, sometimes further than we think we can be pushed, in order to have a faith that is stronger, deeper, and more mature.

Living the Questions

I grew up in a Christian environment. My parents are strong, deeply devoted followers of Jesus, and I went to a Christian school from kindergarten through high school. I grew up reading and learning about the Bible along with a strong set of Christian doctrines and ethics. There is much about those formative years that I would not trade for anything. But it was not until much later in life that I realized that the protective, self-enclosed bubble of that school was an insulating form of religious fundamentalism, in which its convictions about the Christian faith were tightly woven into a narrow ideological and political worldview. Nonetheless, I graduated from that school with a strong faith and an unwavering conviction about my beliefs. The circle of my theology was set.

Then I went to college. It was a small liberal arts school and attending it felt like a culture shock in so many ways. I was a premed/biology major, with intentions of becoming a doctor. In my freshman year biology classes, I learned about evolution and had to demonstrate knowledge and proficiency in an area that up until then I had disdained. I took a class in religious studies, hoping it would resonate with my literalist views of scripture and my fundamentalist views of the faith. Instead, we studied the nature of religious experience by noted thinkers such as William James, Friedrich Schleiermacher, and Sigmund Freud. I turned to the chaplain of my campus ministry for help, only to have him push me with the same kinds of thoughtful, provocative questions that my professors were asking me. The sum effect was that my tightly wound, insulated religious upbringing began to unravel one little thread at a time. The circle of my life experience developed a tension with the circle of my theological worldview.

My dorm situation did not help. The summer before college, I had been praying for a Christian roommate, with whom I could sharpen my faith and deepen my convictions. I had asked Student Affairs to hook me up with a roommate who shared my values, my religious convictions, my major, my study habits, and even my sleeping habits.

They at least got the last one right. We went to bed and woke up at the same time. Otherwise, the housing office managed to find me a roommate who was the complete opposite of me. Our first day on campus, he introduced himself to me by putting several six-packs of beer in my refrigerator. He then marched one woman after another into our room while I was trying to study. He was completely disinterested in matters of the Christian faith.

A few months into college, all of the disillusionment I was experiencing reached a boiling point, and I found myself taking a long walk on campus one night, experiencing a darkness and a fear that characterizes life's toughest moments. I was much like the disciple Andrew that evening, pondering how to respond to Jesus's question, "Magrey, what is it you are looking for?"

The two circles of my life were in complete friction with each other. My theology was not expansive enough to encompass my life experience. My disillusionment could not be explained by the narrow view of my faith. What I was seeking, most of all, was an ease to that tension. I was looking for resonance between my existence and the presence of God.

Discovering the Story
Within My Story

Soon after that long, lonely walk, I was in my dorm room with my Bible open. As I began to pray, a couple of questions drifted into my mind, which I can now say must have come from the Holy Spirit: *"Magrey, with which biblical character can you identify? Whose story in the Bible is becoming your story right now?"*

That kind of earnest listening and prayerful Scripture reading led me to the story of Joseph in Genesis, and I began rereading it with a new interpretive lens. I read it not in an effort to defend myself against the secular threats I was facing, but to locate myself in the possibility of a new, unfolding story that God was just now writing.

I remembered how Joseph was just a young man, perhaps about my age at the time, when he was brutally sold as a slave and whisked away to a foreign land. He was suddenly surrounded by a culture that knew nothing of his faith or his convictions. Joseph's experience in Egypt became the guiding narrative for my first semester in college. I interpreted my struggles in light of his struggles.

In my mind, those things that were tempting me and vying for my attention became the pressures on Joseph to compromise his integrity and conviction. My feelings of loneliness and isolation became the ones that Joseph was experiencing as a slave and, later, in a jail cell, unjustly imprisoned.

I found new life as I read through his story. Joseph's story started to improve the way I saw my situation, leading me to recognize opportunities rather than challenges:

Joseph's rise to preeminence in Egypt inspired me to stay in that college rather than run away, because there was something useful that God was calling me to do there.

Joseph's ultimate forgiveness of his brothers was a stirring reminder to me that what may seem unfair, unjust, or difficult, God might actually use for good.

Joseph's compassion for his fellow inmates and the way he helped them interpret their dreams, and ultimately save many lives in Egypt, showed me how to have compassion for my fellow college students—especially my roommate—and help them experience new life.

One day I went in to talk to my roommate. We had an open, honest conversation where I reiterated some things I appreciated about him, and he of me. We decided to live out the rest of the semester being kind and considerate to each other, and I would temper my instinct to be judgmental and self-righteous about things. Over time, he altered his behavior to accommodate my kindness. No more women in the room. No drinking when I was around. We helped each other with our studies and joined intermural sports teams together. At the end of our first year, after he had decided to transfer to another college, closer to his home, he said to me, "I'm really grateful to have had you as a roommate." The feeling was mutual.

Things improved, but deep down inside I was still searching. Despite my efforts to find other devoted Christians on campus, I entered the spring semester of my freshman year as lonely as ever.

I went home during one school break to revisit my home church to get back in touch with my roots and reconnect with some of the formative people in my faith. Toward the end of high school, I had begun attending a United Methodist congregation whose senior pastor and key staff had already begun to show me a broader, more inclusive approach to the Christian faith. During my spring semester, I reconnected with my senior pastor, one of my favorite people in the world even to this day. I spoke with my youth director and told her what I was feeling. And I spoke to one of my former Sunday school teachers, who listened intently to my struggles and gave me this beautiful word of advice that I remember to this day:

> "Magrey, instead of seeing yourself as the only
> one on that campus, how about seeing yourself
> as just the first one?"

That completely changed my perspective. It was one of those moments when the two circles of my life bent and flexed just enough to accommodate the possibility of a new unfolding reality. The following week, I went to the student affairs office and began the process of starting a new student club, called Cornerstone Student Ministries. I put up signs around campus for a first gathering in my dormitory common room. And wouldn't you know it. That first event brought in a handful of students, none of whom had ever met. All of us were looking for some Christian connection, and they eventually became some of my closest college friends.

Resurrection

The big area of my life that had been feeling the deepest disillusionment—more than angst with my roommate and a desire to meet other Christians—was how my fundamentalist Christian convictions were being challenged to the point of unraveling. I remember one night looking up into the sky, wondering whether God even existed and whether it was any good to pray. I remember realizing I was very close to walking away from the Christian faith entirely.

So, on a second trip to my home church my freshman year, I sat down with my pastor. I shared with him all that I was struggling with in relation to my faith. He listened intently and carefully. Eventually, the subject of the resurrection of Jesus came up, and he suggested to me that God's work of resurrection was not just some singular historical event of the past. It is part of God's ongoing work in the world today, in the lives of people like me. In fact, resurrection is part of the very character of God.

> *The Resurrection is still happening, and you and I see evidence of it all around us, and even within us.*

That was the moment I had been praying for, whether I realized it or not. I came to believe that if the Resurrection were not true, nothing else about my faith, including the existence of God, could be true. I remember in that moment thinking that if someone were to ever produce a body and prove definitively that it was the body of Jesus, that would be the end of my faith. And then, as the years have since rolled by, I've come to believe something even more strongly about the resurrection: The Resurrection is *still* happening, and you and I see evidence of it all around us, and even within us.

Where there is violence, dehumanization, and oppression in the world, God is resurrecting peace with justice, in steady, sometimes subtle ways.

Where there is suffering and heartbreak in our lives—debilitating health, constant anxiety, haunting addiction, residual guilt—God is resurrecting hope and promise in surprising and unmistakable ways.

What I needed, what I was really looking for throughout my tumultuous freshman year of college, was the presence and power of God at work in my life. I needed some way for my two circles to coincide so that my faith and life could coexist within me.

Now, when I open my eyes to the presence and possibility of God and prayerfully seek a resolution to the conflicting circles in my life, I see evidence of the Resurrection. I see it in the lives of people I minister to, in the communities I serve, and even within myself.

It is the Resurrection that, for me, resolved the tension of the two circles and continues to do so to this day. But there was still a lingering question about my vocational calling and career.

Your Mission in Life

By the time I graduated from college, I had earned my bachelor's degree in biology with a premed concentration. But there was a huge stumbling block in the way of my becoming a doctor. Sometimes throughout history, God has spoken to people through a burning bush or a pillar of fire. Sometimes God has spoken through a still, small voice. In my case, God spoke to me in the spring of 1994 through eleven rejection letters from eleven medical schools. I spent much of the next several months pondering my options, which included the possibility of retaking my medical college admissions test and reapplying the next year, as a few of my classmates were determined to do. Or maybe God was calling me into some other career entirely.

I think about this time in my life because it is the kind of episode that many of us go through when we resonate with the question Jesus posed to Andrew and his friend. What is it we are looking for? Many of the hardest moments we go through have to do with our careers, our vocations, and most significantly of all, our callings in life.

A watershed moment in my journey came one day when I walked into my local bookstore and stopped by the section of books called "Career Guides." I thought foolishly that I might find a book that contained all the answers I was looking for regarding my career.

Well, I found one.

You may be familiar with the popular book *What Color Is Your Parachute?* written by Richard Bolles, which details the current state of possible jobs, including trends, income potential, and so on. One day I chanced upon a lesser-known book of his, titled *How to Find Your Mission in Life*. It was very helpful in giving me some clarity that I needed.

According to Bolles, there are three steps to finding your mission in life. The first two are missions for everybody. The last one is exclusively yours.

> 1. *Your first Mission here on Earth* is one which you share with the rest of the human race, but it is no less your individual Mission for the fact

that it is shared: and that is, **to seek to stand
hour by hour in the conscious presence of
God, the one from whom your Mission is
derived.** *The Missioner before the Mission is the
rule.* In religious language, your Mission is: *to
know God, and enjoy Him forever; and to see His
hand in all His works.*

All of us have this mission. We are called to be in a
relationship with God, knowing God, enjoying God, and
seeing God's works throughout the world. That is step one.
If you want to find your mission in life, it starts by being in
a full relationship with God through Jesus Christ. Finding
your purpose in the world is impossible without knowing the
Creator who put you in this world. This is a mission we all
share.

Bolles continues with step two:

2. *Your second Mission here on Earth* is also one
which you share with the rest of the human
race, but it is no less your individual [M]ission
for the fact that it is shared: and that is, **to do
what you can, moment by moment, day by
day, step by step, to make this world a better
place, following the leading and guiding of
God's Spirit within you and around you.**

All of us share this mission too. We are to try to see
God's love made real today. It is the mission of the church,
the community of believers. We are called to work day by day,
hour by hour, step-by-step toward the total transformation
of the community we serve into the God-envisioned kingdom

reality that God intends for it to be. To put it simply and bluntly, we share a mission together to make this world a better place, in line with the kingdom of God.

Then I got to the third point. This was this passage I read in the bookstore that day that hit me squarely between the eyes. It was the answer to Jesus's question to me: "What are you looking for?"

The answer to Bolles's third point is one unique to each of us, and a step we must make on our own:

> 3. *Your third Mission here on Earth* is one which is
> uniquely yours, and that is:
>
> a. **to exercise that Talent which you particu-
> larly came to Earth to use...**
> b. **in those place(s) or setting(s) which God
> has caused to appeal to you the most,**
> c. **and for those purposes which God most
> needs to have done in the world.**[1]

It was in reading that passage that my eyes began to open to the possibility that God was not calling me to be a doctor after all. The most formative, challenging, and transforming aspects of college for me were what I was learning about an expansive, holistic, and healing expression of the Christian faith. God was continuing to unwind my tightly wound fundamentalism and revealing something new and stronger in its place. The call to be a minister was at the intersection of my particular talents, in my most appealing settings, for the greatest needs in the world.

Several weeks later, sitting on Pass-a-Grille Beach in St. Petersburg, Florida, watching the sunset and listening to the waves gently rolling onto shore, I heard the closest thing to an audible voice that I have ever heard from God.

It was the answer to what I was seeking. I heard God say, "Magrey, I want you to be a preacher." And the rest, as they say, is history.

Where Are You Staying?

I can see now that these pivotal moments in my theological journey were driven by questions that Jesus was asking of me. How would I reclaim and reframe the theological foundation from my childhood and adolescence? How would I reconcile that with the emerging needs and hungers of the world? How would I see the Resurrection as the ultimate and ongoing resolution of the two circles of my life? My journey is now a continuous theological project of fusing the best of my Christian upbringing with the "purposes which God most needs to have done in the world."

That kind of resolution leads us to one final, important point as we conclude our study. After Jesus asked Andrew and his friend what they were seeking, they responded with a question of their own: "Rabbi (which is translated *Teacher*), where are you staying?"

What an important question in John's gospel. That word for "staying" is one of John's most significant and most oft-used words. The same word can also mean "abide." The two men were not just asking Jesus where he was going to stay for the night. They were not asking for his home address or his headquarters. They were asking how they might *abide* with him. How they might draw close to him, how they might follow him, and most important, whether Jesus could provide the one thing they were craving and longing for: stability. They were looking for a sense of centeredness and sure-footedness, a grounding and a foundation that would be wide enough and expansive enough to help them make sense of the rapid changes happening in their lives and in the world.

"Rabbi," they asked Jesus, "if you could provide that for us, a sense of stability and home in a world where we feel increasingly like wanderers, we want to be covered in your dust."

"Where are you staying?"

Friends, you and I are going through a time of massive and unprecedented changes in life experience. So much of what you and I may have relied on to provide stability, routine, and comfort seems so unsettled right now. Your circle of life experience may have long been defined by reliance in career advancement, financial stability, reliable relationships, political ideologies, and so much more.

But life happens and that circle has changed, prompting you to hear from Jesus, maybe for the first time, the question that resonates with the deepest part of your spirit. One that a creature can only hear from its Creator, when it is time for one to see God in a new kind of way and to follow with a new kind of intimacy.

What are you seeking? You are seeking a sense of the presence of God.

Where Are You Going?

By the way, the Gospel of John ends with a fascinating twist. In John 13, Jesus gathers with his disciples for the very last conversation they would have before he died. It's the brother of Andrew, Simon Peter, who asked the very same question Andrew did at the beginning of the Gospel. "Lord, where are you going?" (verse 36). Though a different word is used in English, it's the same Greek word for *abide*. Jesus, where are you going to stay?

In response, Jesus said he would go to prepare a place for them—a place with many rooms. That word for *rooms* also comes from the root word for *abide*. It would be a reminder to the disciples that no matter what happens in life, there would always be a way for them to stay close to Jesus. They could always be close enough to be covered by the dust of their Messiah.

He told them this around a table, in which he blessed, broke, and gave bread that would remind them of his presence. He would pour, lift, and bless, a cup that would remind them of his love. It would be in this act of remembrance that they could always turn to abide in the presence and love of Jesus with them.

Friends, come to Jesus with your questions. As Rabbi Abraham Heschel said, "We are closer to God when we are asking questions than when we think we have all the answers." Let those questions draw you to a closer, more intimate connection with God. Allow those questions to stretch and mature your faith, to ease the tensions with your life experience.

Ultimately, may you be covered by the dust of the rabbi, so that the love and grace of God can fill you with a constant, abiding, and steady sense of the presence of Jesus with you.

Questions for Reflection

1. How would you respond to Jesus's question: "What are you looking for?"

2. When have you experienced a time when your theology has had to grow and expand in order to make sense of the changes in your life? How painful was that experience? What helped you through it?

3. How are Richard Bolles's three steps in finding your mission helpful to you?

4. What would abiding in Jesus look like for you?

ACKNOWLEDGMENTS

Writing the last chapter of this book filled me with memories of many people who played a critical role in nurturing my life through that season of disillusionment and doubt. These are individuals whose paths intersected with mine at just the right time, to offer loving support and provocative ideas that guided me into a fuller, more expansive, and more robust relationship with Jesus Christ. It is to these people that I dedicate this book, with profound gratitude.

The Reverend Dr. John A. Stroman was my senior pastor at Pasadena Community Church in St. Petersburg, Florida, and is a dear friend and mentor to this day. Nancy Gilson was my youth director, and she and her husband, Mike, have been supportive and loving throughout my ministry. I give thanks for Dr. Akma Adam, who during my years at Eckerd College, taught "Introduction to Religious Studies" and "New Testament Greek" and showed me the value of a rigorous, intellectual approach to the Christian faith. Rev. Fitz Connor was my director of campus ministries, and his weekly lunchtime Bible studies on campus gave me permission and language to ask questions of Christianity that I had been longing to ask but was afraid to.

I am indebted to United Theological Seminary and the amazing teaching of its Bible and theology professors. Dr. Tom Boomershine, Dr. Kathy Farmer, and Dr. Tom Dozeman opened my eyes to an invigorating, critical view of the Scriptures. Dr. Carolyn Bohler showed me how to integrate process theology with the work of pastoral care. Dr. Kendall McCabe showed me how to lead the work of worship with integrity, creativity, and faithfulness to tradition. And Dr. Tyron Inbody was the most formative in expanding my capacity as a theologian to think, reflect, construct, and apply the richness of the Christian faith. I cannot imagine doing what I am doing without each of their influences on my life.

I have been blessed over the years to serve some amazing congregations filled with laity and clergy who have ministered to me as much as anything I have hoped to offer them. I am grateful for the people of St. Paul's United Methodist Church in Cherokee, Iowa, and people like Rich, John, Andrea, and Jan Cook, who embody the kind of love, joy, and laughter that will forever mark my spiritual journey. I am grateful for the laity and clergy of Hyde Park United Methodist Church, including my fellow clergy, Sally Campbell-Evans, Vicki Walker, and Justin LaRosa. I am privileged to serve among amazing staffers, including Peggy Hisey, Dr. Michael Dougherty, Mat Hotho, Colleen Schmitt, Meagan Kempton, John Barolo, Lynn Osborne, Rich Allen, and countless others.

There is no way I could do the work of ministry without my clergy covenant group: Craig Hammond, Cameron Lashbrook, David Miller, Brett Opalinski, Steve Price, Scott Smith, Roy Terry, and David Williamson. Our care and support of each other through the highs and lows of ministry has been an enduring gift. You all make me a better person and a more effective minister. Other clergy have served as invaluable mentors along my journey: Steve Bennett, Jim Harnish, Bernie Lieving, Dr. Steve Harper, and Bishop Ken Carter.

This book along with most of the other books I have written have come from the generous invitation and contribution of the fine people at Abingdon Press. I am grateful for Susan Salley, along with my friend and editor, Brian Sigmon. He always has a way of making my writing sharper and clearer.

Finally, I cannot imagine life without the love and support of my family. My brothers, Genniser and Mykel; their spouses, Amanda and Sara; and their children: thank you for who you are, and for the moments we share together. To my parents, Mike and Tessie, thank you for the self-sacrifice and generosity you have always shown to help me be the best person I can be. And to Grace and Maddy, what can I say? It will always be my greatest honor to be your dad. I'll try not to embarrass you too much.

NOTES

Introduction

1   "The History of the Question Mark," Historically Irrelevant, accessed October 4, 2022, https://historicallyirrelevant.com /post/3708038709/the-history-of-the-question-mark.

2   Danah Zohar and Dr. Ian Marshall, *SQ: Connecting with Our Spiritual Intelligence* (New York: Bloomsbury, 2000), 15.

3   Martin B. Copenhaver, *Jesus Is the Question: The 307 Questions Jesus Asked and the 3 He Answered* (Nashville: Abingdon Press, 2014), xix.

4   *Three Types of Questions*, accessed October 4, 2022, https://www.umasd.org/cms/lib7/PA01000379/ Centricity/Domain/518/Documents/Three%20Types %20of%20Questions.pdf.

Chapter One

1   John Wesley, "Wesley's Covenant Service, Directions for Renewing Our Covenant with God," in *John and Charles Wesley: Selected Prayers, Hymns, Journal Notes, Sermons, Letters and Treatises,* ed. Frank Whaling (New York: Paulist, 1981), 142.

2   Robert L. Kinast, *Let Ministry Teach: A Guide to Theological Reflection* (Collegeville, MN: The Liturgical Press, 1996).

3   Will Ferrell, *Talladega Nights: The Ballad of Ricky Bobby* (Sony, 2006).

4   Peter Gomes, *The Scandalous Gospel of Jesus: What's So Good About the Good News?* (New York: HarperOne, 2007), 69.

Chapter Two

1   Christina Rossetti, "Judge Not According to the Appearance," in *The Poetical Works of Christina Georgina Rossetti*, ed. William Michael Rossetti (New York: Macmillan, 1906), 231.

2   Sharon Ellison, "How Can Simple Curious Questions Have Such Disarming Power?" March 8, 2013, YouTube video, 4:10, https://www.youtube.com/watch?v=1WB9rD25lzk.

3   Pema Chödrön, *When Things Fall Apart: Heart Advice for Difficult Times* (Boston: Shambhala, 1997), 41–42.

4   Sarah Fielding, "New Study Shows 91 Percent of Fears Don't Come True," *Best Life*, August 8, 2019, https://bestlifeonline .com/anxiety-vs-reality-study/.

5   John Wesley, *Rev. John Wesley's Journal*, January 25, 1736, in *The Works of the Rev. John Wesley*, vol. 1 (Philadelphia: D. and S. Neall and W. S. Stockton, 1826), 126.

6   Wesley, 127.

7   Horatio G. Spafford, "It Is Well with My Soul," music by Philip P. Bliss, *The United Methodist Hymnal* (Nashville: The United Methodist Publishing House, 1989), 377, stanza 1.

8   Katharina von Schlegel, "Be Still, My Soul," trans. Jane Borthwick, music by Jean Sibelius, *The United Methodist Hymnal* (Nashville: The United Methodist Publishing House, 1989), , 534, stanza 2.

9   Wesley, *Rev. John Wesley's Journal*, 126–27.

Chapter Three

1   James Nestor, *Breath: The New Science of a Lost Art* (New York: Riverhead Books, 2020), xix.

2   Nestor, 177–78.

3   Nestor, 212.

4   Based on and adapted from Patricia D. Brown, *Paths to Prayer: Finding Your Own Way to the Presence of God* (New York: Jossey-Bass, 2003), 113–18.

5   Diana Butler Bass, *Grateful: The Subversive Practice of Giving Thanks* (New York: HarperOne, 2018), 86.

6   Bass, 79.

7   Steve Harper, *Five Marks of a Methodist: The Fruit of a Living Faith* (Nashville: Abingdon, 2015), 27–28.

Chapter Four

1   *Poetic Words of Ralph Waldo Emerson: 4000+ words of the Transcendentalist* (N.p.: UB Tech, 2016), 18.

2   Adapted from Carlos Wilton, *Lectionary Preaching Workbook: For All Users of the Revised Common, the Roman Catholic, and the Episcopal Lectionaries* (Lima, OH: CSS, 2004), 48.

3   Augustine, *The Confessions 1.1*, trans. Maria Boulding (New York: Vintage, 1997), 3.

4   Stuart K. Hine, "How Great Thou Art," *The United Methodist Hymnal* (Nashville: The United Methodist Publishing House, 1989), 77, refrain.

5   Friedrich Nietzsche, *Beyond Good and Evil*, trans. Helen Zimmern (N.p.: Millennium, 2014), 46.

6   Augustine, *The Confessions*, 7.12.28.

7   Penn Jillette, "Penn Says?—A Gift of the Bible," July 8, 2010, YouTube video, 2:22, https://www.youtube.com /watch?v=6md638smQd8

8   Ben McConnell and Jackie Huba, *Creating Customer Evangelists: How Loyal Customers Become a Volunteer Sales Force* (Chicago: Dearborn Trade, 2013), 13.

9   Marjorie Hewitt Suchocki, *In God's Presence: Theological Reflections on Prayer* (St. Louis: Chalice, 1996), 4.

Notes

Chapter Five

1   Lao-Tse, *The Tao Teh King, or the Tao and Its Characteristics*, trans. James Legge, part. 2, 49.2, in *Sacred Books Of The Daoism, Confucianism, Buddhism: Tao Te Ching, Chuang Tzu, Analects, The Dhammapada. Classics of Eastern Philosophy* (N.p.: Strelbytskyy Multimedia Publishing, 2020).

2   See *Sahih Muslim* (Book 1, Number 72). Anas ibn Malik (612-709) heard Muhammad make this statement.

3   Marriott International. "Golden Rule." Television advertisement. mcgarrybowen, 2017, https://www.youtube .com/watch?v=62cs2M4L5k0.

4   See "Heineken Worlds Apart Open Your World 1," YouTube video, 4:25, posted by Aaron Whittier, April 26, 2017, https://youtu.be/dKggA9k8DKw.

5   Kate Murphy, "A Chat with Maya Angelou," *New York Times*, April 21, 2013. https://www.nytimes.com/2013/04/21 /opinion/sunday/a-chat-with-maya-angelou.html.

6   The following interpretation is adapted from Walter Wink, "Beyond Just War and Pacifism: Jesus' Nonviolent Way," CRES (Center for Religious Experience and Study), accessed October 7, 2022, http://www.cres.org/star/_wink.htm.

7   Heidi Fenton, "Emotions Run High as Takunda Mavima Is Sent to Prison for Crash Killing Wyoming Students," mLive Michigan, September 10, 2012, https://www.mlive .com/news/grand-rapids/2012/09/emotions_run_high_as _takunda_m.html.

8   Takunda Mavima, interview on "Feel Like You Belong," YouTube video, 22:55, October 26, 2015, https://www .youtube.com/watch?v=8eaStRFprRg&t=105s.

9   Chris McGreal, "Forgiveness, peace at Wisconsin vigil,"
     The Hindu, published August 9, 2012, updated July 1, 2016.
     https://www.thehindu.com/opinion/op-ed/forgiveness
     -peace-at-wisconsin-vigil/article3742957.ece

Chapter Six

1   Richard Nelson Bolles, *How to Find Your Mission in Life*, rev.
     ed. (New York: Ten Speed Press, 2005), 11–12.

Watch videos based on *Questions Jesus Asked* with Magrey R. deVega through Amplify Media.

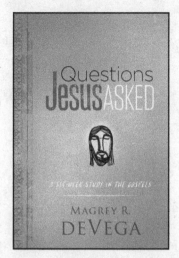